AN INTRODUCTION TO ROBERT FROST

An Introduction

to

Robert Frost

Elizabeth Isaacs

HASKELL HOUSE PUBLISHERS LTD.
Publishers of Scarce Scholarly Books
NEW YORK, N. Y. 10012
1972

HASKELL HOUSE PUBLISHERS Ltd.

Publishers of Scarce Scholarly Books

280 LAFAYETTE STREET

NEW YORK. N. Y. 10012

Library of Congress Cataloging in Publication Data

Isaacs, Emily Elizabeth, 1917-
   An introduction to Robert Frost.

   Bibliography: p.
   1. Frost, Robert, 1874-1963.
PS3511.R94Z75 1972   811'.5'2   72-4617
ISBN 0-8383-1593-3

Printed in the United States of America

To my encouraging family and friends

Acknowledgments

I am deeply indebted to Washington University and to Cornell College for providing time and fellowship funds for this study. Special thanks go to Professor Jarvis Thurston, Washington University, who directed the original research; and to Dean Howard Troyer, Cornell College, who encouraged its completion. Invaluable assistance was given by Professor Winifred Van Etten, Cornell College, who edited the manuscript; and by Professor Agnes Sibley, Lindenwood College, who prepared the typescript.

Preface

"Seek not in me the big I capital
Nor yet the little dotted in me seek."
—"Iota Subscript"

In his eighty-eighth year Robert Frost has had wide recognition. He has travelled half way around the world, met the public in lecture performances on several continents, represented the arts as senior poet at the inauguration of the President of the United States, talked informally to students in colleges and universities across the nation, challenged the press in newspapers and on television, promoted the cause of poetry by auction of his manuscripts, recorded wide selections of his poetry, starred in a documentary movie, published a new book, and received the Congressional Medal. His diverse activities indicate the wide acclaim accorded this "dean of American poetry," who for twenty years tried unsuccessfully to market his first volume. In the half century between his first and his latest public readings, the status of the man has changed; the personality remains unchanged. His careers of teaching, lecturing, and writing have all reached fruition. Today he maintains a laconic, wistful relativism in a world which he still finds more good than bad; and he continues from time to time to add one more poetic comment on it.

In spite of his current popularity, the poet Robert Frost has had very little serious consideration from professional critics and very little real understanding from his many readers. Contemporary critics, until very recently, have tended to dismiss him as "happy farmer," "bucolic sage," or "platitudinous philosopher." There has been very little real critical analysis of Frost's poetry—partly the result, perhaps, of Frost's own stated disapproval of explication. He seems to contemporary critics stubbornly unaware of the values of analytic criticism. To his misfortune, he is often overpraised by journalistic critics and by amateur poets who are less able to stand the test of close reading than he.

Perhaps one of the basic reasons for the tendency to neglect a critical consideration of Frost's poetry has been the recent dominance of the T. S. Eliot school in which the poet serves as both poet *and* critic. In this school of modern criticism the metaphysical tradition has held; and Frost has not been the subject of essays from the *avant-garde* analysts who prefer complex, esoteric subjects. Frost himself has refused to clarify his own poetry with long prose commentaries as many of these poets do; and he has not tried to clarify any other poet's works as some critic-poets do.

When he has indulged in a few prose pieces, he has often added to the misunderstanding of himself and his poetry by his own paradoxical and metaphorical remarks. Although he has often talked about his "theory of poetry," he is actually an unsystematic theorist, neither clear nor precise, who seems carried away by his own provocative phrasing when he writes prose or talks about poetry. He seems a poet's "critic," whose ideas are most meaningful to those who already know the poetic experience. His "theory" is best understood, not from his prose essays, but as it is revealed in his poetry. Here he is a complete master of his medium.

Frost's double role as dean of popular poetry and as artist of more serious intent is reflected in the unbalanced quality and quantity of writing about him. Individual volumes about Frost to date have been limited to four biographical sketches, five critical studies, and two collections of essays: one printed by his publisher on the anniversary of his twenty-fifth year as poet, and the other selected from more recent periodicals.[1] There are, of course, hundreds of eulogies of Frost in popular magazines; there are only a few perceptive articles in academic journals and in "little magazines." With a similar lack of balance, a few of his poems are published over and over in high school texts and pocket editions; most of his best work remains unread except by those who examine its versatility in the individual volumes or in *The Complete Poems* (1949). It is encouraging to note that critics like Allen Tate and Randall Jarrell are beginning to show more interest and respect than in the past. Mr. Tate has introduced Frost's poetry in an anthology as that of a man "who has produced a body of poetry as impressive as any in English of our time."[2] Yet it would seem to the careful reader that seldom has man or poetry been so misunderstood.

It is the purpose of this book to provide a synthesis of the current basic information that may bring a better understanding of Frost's work. The first section will summarize the scattered biographical materials and will conclude with a survey of contrasting attitudes taken toward this personality during the half-century of his publication. The second section will consider his poetic credo and practices as they are informally definable from a general study of his *Complete Poems* and from his prose essays. The last section will present explications of a dozen poems which have been carefully selected to represent some of the best of Frost's work in lyric, dramatic, and satiric forms. An evaluative conclusion will attempt to define the position of poet and poetry in the literary world today.

In the final analysis, any book about Robert Frost must admit to being only "an introduction." At the end of a year when this enigmatic octogenarian has received more publicity than any other American writer and has reached the peak of his poetic production, it seems fitting that the man and his art be discussed in an introductory, rather than a conclusive volume. He himself, at age eighty-eight, in the final poem of his new book leaves the door wide open for things to come:

> I see in Nature no defeat
> In one tree's overthrow
> Or for myself in my retreat
> For yet another blow.[3]

Contents

Part One

The Poet

"They would not find me changed from him they knew
Only more sure of all I thought was true."

—"Into My Own."

Chapter One

Biographical Backgrounds

A tradition involving both the adventurous and the academic has characterized the life of Robert Frost from its early backgrounds to the present. He traces his surname back to the ninth-century Danish invasion of England and his immediate family to one Henry Frost, who helped found St. John's College at Cambridge. His family's history in New England begins with Nicholas Frost, a Puritan who brought the line to America in 1632. Nine generations later, Robert's paternal grandfather, William Prescott Frost, established the family in Lawrence, Massachusetts, where he farmed and worked as overseer in a mill. He and his wife, one of the early feminists in America, were strong-minded parents with great ambition for their only son, whom they sent to Harvard to become a lawyer. However, William Prescott Jr. revolted against their plans for his future and fled from the parochial, provincial traditions of New England. While teaching for an interval in Pennsylvania, he married Belle Moodie; together they went to California in search of a new life. She was a Scottish refugee teacher with imaginative Swedenborgian tendencies; her husband was an aloof political radical. Their son, Robert Lee Frost, was born in San Francisco on March 26, 1874. (Even the date of the poet's birth was for years mistaken. Robert himself had believed it to be 1875, and the United States Senate proclaimed an official celebration of his 75th birthday in 1950. Shortly thereafter an old letter from his father was found in the Harvard Alumni Office announcing Robert's birth in 1874. The poet is said to have accepted his added year with the laconic remark, "He should know!") Robert Frost has said that he was shaped by the unorthodoxies of his parental background, retaining his mother's poetic mysticism and his father's independent spirit.[1]

The poet has cherished stories of his family's early life in the western frontier town. The father edited a progressive Democratic newspaper, *The Bulletin,* which regularly carried his radical editorials as well as occasional poems and critical reviews by his wife. He was an intense

Copperhead and States Rights man, true "Sep-a-ra-tist" according to the poet. Though too young to fight in the Civil War and disappointed at its outcome, he named his only son in honor of its hero. He became a plunger in the San Francisco stock market, carried a gun, and campaigned in political battles. At home, he seemed a sardonic man, who had only an erratic interest in his children. Robert Frost remembers only their silent occasional walks together along the Pacific beaches, where they shot at bottles in the surf, and their frequent trips through San Francisco saloons where the boy's duties were to distribute campaign literature. He both feared and respected this grim father, who early brought a sense of tragedy into his life.[2]

The mother seems to have been much closer to Robert and his younger sister, Jeanie, than the father was. She read to the children, provided them with imaginative games, and gave them a sense of family security and religious fervor that they missed in their silent agnostic father. Frost's father dreamed of trips "to the islands" as a cure for his developing tuberculosis, but eventually died of it in 1885. Mrs. Frost, impoverished by his illness and extravagances, was forced to return to her husband's family in New England.[3]

It is difficult to assess the exact influence of this early period on the poet's later work. Frost has identified certain of his poems as "Californian" in image and source. He calls *A Further Range*, "my secretly published book about California," and "Neither Out Far Nor In Deep," "one of my California poems." Although only a decade in length, this California interval had its later influence in his life and poetry. He has returned there frequently in his maturity and has authorized a collection of his manuscripts for the University of California.[4] It was in California, at age ten, that he had written his first story—a kind of serial which he later continued in New England. It contained a dramatic symbol which has occasionally reappeared in his later poetry: a lost forgotten tribe, safe in its withdrawal, living in a ravine somewhere unknown to the rest of the world (cf. "A Drumlin Woodchuck," "Into My Own"). Years later, the poet said that he often put himself to sleep by dreaming of "this inaccessible, happy tribe defending itself against all disturbances and confusion."[5] In a recent lecture, he cited three other poems that portray this continued love of seclusion which he has called his "triple theme song": "Stopping by Woods on a Snowy Evening," "The Road Not Taken," and "Come In."[6] The theme of isolation has been consistent in his poetry from his earliest manuscripts to the present.

The transition from California was difficult for the entire family; but eventually the young Frost developed a kind of transplanted love for the locale of his ancestors. He became a good student in the Lawrence schools, read eagerly in local libraries, and with the encouragement of his mother went rapidly through the traditional poets of New England.

14

His first poem, "La Noche Triste," written in 1890, was published in the *Lawrence High School Bulletin* in April of that year. This publication was followed by some ventures into historical essay writing and the composition of the class hymn to be sung to a Beethoven melody.[7] Upon graduation, he shared honors in his class with Elinor White and delivered the valedictory address which she helped him write. Of these years Frost has said, "I wanted only two things—to write a few poems and to marry Elinor." Three years later they were married, "in a union of singular idyllic beauty."[8]

By the time of his marriage, he had already written some of the poems that were to appear twenty years later in *A Boy's Will;* and a thin volume of some of his early poetry, *Twilight,* was privately printed in 1894. (A single copy of this rare book brought $3500.00 at public auction in 1950!) His first national publication was a poem, "My Butterfly," in the November, 1894, *Independent Magazine,* whose editor admired it for its "Lanier-like qualities." Frost has said that in two lines of this poem, written at age fifteen, he first caught what he thought he was after:

> The grey grass is scarce dappled with the snow;
> Its two banks have not shut upon the river.

In discussing this first recognition of the truly poetic moment, he has said, "It's a funny thing when you first know poetry has come from you as I did in these lines . . . it's like tears inside."[9] Though he has since discarded many of his early poems as not worthy of republication, he has been consistently fond of this first effort: "These were the lines that set me on my way. That's why I kept this poem for my first book"[10] One poet-critic who read it wrote to Frost's editor commending the young poet's "secret of genius." He also warned Frost, however, of the probable disappointment if he dared contemplate the writing of poetry as a livelihood and urged him to learn a trade or a profession.[11] Characteristically. Frost paid little attention to either his editor's or his critic's opinion.

This independence of spirit shows in his relations with his grandfather, who also recommended that he pursue a more practical vocation. With the hope that he would study for the law like his father, this grandfather sent him to Dartmouth; but the curriculum bored Frost, and he left college with the excuse of having to help his mother as a teacher of Latin.

During the next three years, he worked at many odd jobs, travelled about the country, and absorbed a variety of experiences which were to be utilized in his later poetry. He read constantly and without plan as he travelled and worked sporadically as bobbin boy at his grandfather's mill. as shoemaker, as journalist, and as itinerant handy-man on a tramping tour of the South. His favorites in the classics of literature were absorbed during these years, he says: Shakespeare, Homer, and Virgil. He became more and more determined to cling to his original vague belief that artistic achievement was what he wanted in life in spite of its precarious possibility for him.[12]

Some of his later poems seem to have come from the impressions of this later period: "In a Disused Graveyard," where his grandparents were buried; "A Lone Striker," from his years at the mill; "The Quest of the Purple-Fringed," from his travels and botanical interests. Early vignettes from his feature column in *The Lawrence Sentinel* show a sensitive sympathy to the world about him.[13]

At twenty-three years of age, encouraged by his wife and grandfather, he entered Harvard as an irregular undergraduate. He is said to have been drawn there by what he had heard of its great teachers: Irving Babbitt, George Santayana, and William James. He has said that there he learned that "all thinking was not something which *had* been done; it was something being done in immediate and continuous activity."[14] At Harvard, he also found classical confirmation for his practice of metrics and diction, which he later called "the sound of sense." ("I first heard the voice of the printed page from a Virgilian *Eclogue,* from Homer's *Odyssey,* and from *Hamlet.*"[15]) He listened with keen ear to the Latin and Greek of Babbitt and to the philosophy lectures of Santayana, "whose golden speech impressed me with its deliberate speed and mental exposition of brilliance."[16]

His university career lasted only one year, however; he refused to be bound to an academic discipline that seemed to him dogmatic and illogical. He was more interested in his extracurricular conversations with a local grass-roots philosopher named Charley Hall, "whose speech had a racy commonness and whose talks were more stimulating for their homely shrewdness than the lectures of the correct college instructors."[17] During his conversations with Hall, Frost says he began to wonder why a good listener could not write poetry like this, recording in his mind the natural rhythms and sounds of this man's speech. His interest in creative writing grew; and finally, he deserted journalism, manual labor, teaching, and college—all roads not taken./ At the turn of the century he began seriously to consider the writing of poetry as his real profession, as a way of life close to the soil he loved and to the turn of talk and thought found there. At about this same time, failing health seemed to indicate the possibility of tuberculosis; and he was ordered by his doctor to get some sort of outdoor occupation.

His grandfather, determined to have him make some practical decision, bought him a farm near Derry, New Hampshire. There he settled the family of four, allowing Robert to "take one year and try poetry . . ." If this did not work, he was to devote himself to the single occupation of

16

farming from then on. Frost's response to this ultimatum was characteristic: "Give me *twenty* years!" And it was exactly twenty years before his first real book of poetry was published.[18]

To be a farmer and a poet on the edge of conservative Derry was hard for Frost in those first years. The neighbors were astounded by the unorthodoxy of his farming; they observed him doing much of his work at night and writing poetry or walking in the woods with his children by day. Profits were slight, but the local merchants were usually willing to extend credit to this poet-farmer whom they couldn't help liking in spite of his "different" ways. After six years of desultory farm life, he was stricken by a severe attack of pneumonia, and for a while there was good reason to fear that he would not recover.[19]

In spite of physical hardships, these Derry years seem to have been poetically productive, for the backgrounds and germs of many of the *Complete Poems* are here. (One such early poem was printed later in a more complex revision: "The Tuft of Flowers" from "The Quest of the Purple-Fringed.") Certain poems reflect the constant demands of the rocky farm and the growing family upon his health and the precious time that he tried to keep for his writing. (See "Black Cottage.") His wife, ever sympathetic, encouraged him to write in spite of the necessary financial sacrifices involved in such a decision. Frost has told his bibliographers that some poems in his first two volumes, *A Boy's Will* and *North of Boston,* are reminiscent of this locale and his moods there. Particularly, he has said of his first poem in *A Boy's Will* ("Into My Own"), "Here is the beginning of my desire to hide from something."[20] In it he recreates the image of his first short story written as a boy in California.

To be a farmer and a poet demanded stamina and courage. To be a teacher and a poet would be easier for Frost. Having interested a local trustee of the Pinkerton Academy by reading some of his poetry at a church dinner, Frost was offered a job as English teacher in that highly respected cultural center of conservative Derry, where his teaching proved almost as unorthodox as his farming. He has since told of his experiences there, "rattling the windows the first few periods of every day and then sodjering a little."[21] He taught at Pinkerton for five years: Latin, Greek, English literature, and composition. His classes were conducted with the easy informality that has characterized his teaching ever since: a combination of reading and talking, but never lecturing formally. His lack of respect for such traditions as the daily chapel service at Pinkerton was offset by the constructive influence he had on his students, who played football with him or followed him on long walks through the woods, discussing everything from classical literature and astronomy to sports and current theatre. He used his classes for oral criticism of his students' creative writing; he advised the school newspaper in a liberal

17

manner; he coached plays that had never before been presented at Pinkerton: Marlowe's *Dr. Faustus,* Milton's *Comus,* Yeats' *Land of Heart's Desire.* He introduced his students to readings from Shaw's *Arms and the Man* and Synge's *Playboy of the Western World.* At his farm house, he entertained his favorite students during long evenings around his fireside with literary and philosophical discussions.[22]

Eventually, his reputation as a teacher came to the attention of the state authorities, and he was asked to lecture at educational conventions and to conduct teaching demonstrations. For this purpose he developed his famous classifications for his young writers' subject matter. These have eventually been incorporated as an integral part of Frost's own *ars poetica* as he has developed himself as a professional poet:

> Uncommon in experience—uncommon in writing
> Common in experience—common in writing
> Uncommon in experience—common in writing
> Common in experience—uncommon in writing

He continues to admonish himself as well as all would-be writers to use the last variety of criteria.

His students recall that his informal conversations were as unconventional as his teaching and as definite in preferences for subject matter. A portrait by an early pupil indicates the same traits of personality that have been characteristic of Frost through the years:

There was always an abundance of conversation but almost never any argument. Frost never argued. He knew what he knew, and never had any interest arguing about it. In the same way he was always willing to let others think what they wanted to think. He had a Woodrow Wilson sense of loyalty. I never knew a person who was more sensitive to slights, rebuffs, and acts of unfriendliness than Frost, or who seemed to carry the scar of them longer, and I have never met one whose loyalty was more thoroughly the lasting kind.[23]

Frost's success at Derry led to his promotion to the State Normal School at Plymouth, New Hampshire. Though he taught psychology to the young ladies there only one year, the period provided for him an important development. He established the informal pattern in educational and social situations which still characterizes him, and he spent a good deal of time in self-analysis and philosophical conversation with his friend Sidney Cox, who was then teaching in the local high school.[24] Cox says Frost's courses at Plymouth defied the prescribed state course of study by substituting Plato's *Republic* and Rousseau's *Emile* as texts. He recounts a conversation concerning Whitman and Shakespeare which reveals Frost's faith in emotional education through poetry. He recalls that Frost's favorite authors at this time were Matthew Arnold, Mark Twain, Stevenson, Hawthorne, and H. G. Wells. He remembers Frost's curiosity about the world of nature, his agility and interest in sports, his denial of formal religion, and always his complete simplicity and sincerity of spirit:

It is true that when I met him in 1911 . . . I first thought him uncouth. We were at a school dance where both of us were against the wall, and he wore an unpressed suit and a gray, soft-collared shirt; and he sat with crossed knees and poked fun. . . When I walked with him, I felt the world growing larger and stronger, and more challenging in his company. I detected in his speech what seemed to be a lack of elegance and in his attitude an absence of conformity. There was something earthy and imperfectly tamed about him.[25]

Some of his recent critics have said that this Derry-Plymouth period was a crystalizing one in both the life and poetry of Robert Frost. Throughout his later life, he has continued to do a little farming, some teaching, and much writing, just as he did there in his early days. Once annually during these years he would send off a packet of his poems to literary magazines he respected: *Scribners, Century,* and *The Atlantic Monthly.* Once a year they would all reject the "stark, unmelodious verses." In no way deterred from his original course (he had asked for twenty years for his poetry), Frost was willing to wait. He managed in the twenty years to publish a dozen short pieces in scattered, rather unimportant periodicals; but he was never acknowledged as a first-rate poet with a full volume to his credit until his migration from New to Old England.

After a year at Plymouth, Frost decided the time for change had come. His family discussed the relative merits of Canada or England and chose the latter, where they hoped to live in a thatched cottage at low cost and find a more receptive audience for poetry. They moved to England in the fall of 1912, the year Harriet Monroe founded *Poetry Magazine* in Chicago, a magazine that was later to give him his first important recognition and later still to profit from the auction of his early manuscripts.

The English artists and critics of that day were more receptive and progressive than those of the still lethargic American literary scene. Prominent in this more vital, creative society was another American, Ezra Pound, who provided the earliest and most important literary contact of Frost's career. Frost had settled his family at Beaconsfield in Buckinghamshire where he hoped to continue to write and eventually to publish. One evening, sitting before his fire sorting his poems, he told his wife that he thought he'd "run up to London with a few verses" that seemed to make a good sequence for a book.[26] Ignoring several well-known publishers who demanded subsidy for original manuscripts, he took his verses to the house of David Nutt and was surprised to have his manuscript accepted three days later. In an equally casual fashion, he happened in on a poetry reading at the Harold Monro Bookshop one evening and met F. S. Flint, who recognized him as American by his shoes and asked him if he were a writer. Flint at this time was interested in the French Symbolistes and their relation to the new Imagist school in England. The two men conversed about poetry and publications, and Flint suggested that he put Frost in touch with Pound, then prominent in the English literary reviews. Moreover, Pound, as foreign correspondent, was making recommendations for *Poetry* magazine and was advising its editor, Miss Monroe. Frost eventually received a postcard on which was printed "E. Pound. At home, sometimes." He waited several months to call until the day his proofsheets of *A Boy's Will* were to come from the printer, then went round to see the critic. Pound went with him to get the sheets, read them twice, dismissed the poet hastily, and then proceeded to write a very favorable review and a letter of recommendation for publication in the next issue of *Poetry*.[27] The very "setness" to which Frost's first publisher twenty years before had objected was warmly praised by this more astute critic, who recognized a new style and technique in this "very American verse." Pound's predictions were based soundly on Frost's "honest writing," and he lamented the lack of taste in editors who had rejected him:

It is a sinister thing that so American, I might say so parochial a talent as that of Robert Frost should have to be exported before it can find encouragement or recognition. . . Mr. Frost is an honest writer, from his knowledge and his emotions; not simply picking up the manner which magazines are accepting at the moment and applying it to topics in vogue. . . His is the work of a man who will make no concessions or pretences.[28]

Pound was eager to claim new poets for his own "schools" (Imagism, Vorticism, etc.); he introduced Frost at luncheons, salons, and "Tuesday Evenings" at T. E. Hulme's as his own new find. He got Harold Monro to publish two new Frost poems in *Poetry Review*. In 1915, *The Atlantic Monthly* was sufficiently convinced of its original error to give him American publication of "Birches," "The Sound of Trees," and "The Road Not Taken."[29] But relations between Pound and Frost—two strong, independent thinkers—did not last long. Pound demanded disciples; though Frost was interested and appreciative, he did not relish such a restricted association. Instead, he leased a farm near the "Georgian" group in Gloucestershire and enjoyed a simple life with such neighbors as Wilfred Gibson, Lascelles Abercrombie, John Drinkwater, Rupert Brook, and his particular friend, Edward Thomas. Their learned conversations about life and literature and their leisurely pace pleased Frost more than the frenetic dynamism of Pound in London. These friendships are memorialized in Gibson's poem "A Golden Room," and Frost himself wrote "The Road Not Taken" as a tribute to Thomas, who was later killed in the war. When Frost decided to return to America in 1915 after the outbreak of the war, he brought Thomas's son home with him.[30]

Frost returned to his native country to find himself recognized as a full-fledged poet. It had taken the full twenty years that he had demanded of his grandfather for the success of his poetry. Upon his return, a critic wrote of him, "It seems to me that this poet is destined to take a permanent place in American literature."[31] The predicition had been made for his future, and he was finally on the way to his original goal. Shortly after his arrival in New York, he was surprised to find Amy Lowell's review of North of Boston in a new magazine called The New Republic. He was even more surprised to find that he had an American publisher, Henry Holt. Mrs. Holt, who had been a long-time admirer of Frost, had urged her husband to import A Boy's Will from David Nutt. As a result, Holt had fought and won a legal battle with Nutt over the rights to North of Boston, which sold a phenomenal twenty thousand copies in America.[32] Hardly able to believe his good fortune and his new fame, Frost settled his family unobtrusively on a small farm near Franconia, New Hampshire.

Here he was visited by a young student of the "new poetry," Joseph Warren Beach, who has written an interesting portrait of Frost in 1915:

I have a very vivid memory of Frost at this time . . . when I first became aware of the new poets and their actions. They were all about forty, but they were almost all taking their first serious steps in poetic art and just becoming visible on the literary horizon. I called on Frost at his farmhouse in Franconia. . . Frost seemed very glad to welcome a young professor who was interested in his poetry. He didn't appear to be very busy on his farm. . . I came every day for nearly a week to spend the whole day with the Frosts. Mrs. Frost provided luncheon and coffee, and the rest of the time we spent up on a hill in the hemlock trees or in the barn sitting on the floor under the haymow. I remember Frost's eyes peering out speculatively from among the strands of hay that hung down in his face. During my stay there, three old pupils of his from the Normal School came to see him. . . In our philosophic discussions around the table we had the admiring audience of Mrs. Frost and two of the young children, who had the bright eyes of young animals and the high brows of genus homo. . . In our more private talks we discussed life and poetry. He was full of the English poets of the time, whom he had known personally and whose work he discussed with fine appreciation, but also with cool objectivity, discrimination, and detachment. We also discussed the English classics. He was not enthusiastic about Milton, for he did not hear the sound of the human voice in his rolling lines. His favorite poets were Chaucer, Shakespeare, Wordsworth, and Browning. For in their verse he could hear the inflections of the voice speaking.[33]

Recognition came fast after that transitional summer in 1915, and for forty-seven years the career of Frost in America has successfully combined writing, teaching, and lecturing throughout the country. Though he has always called New England his home, he has left it for long periods as poet-in-residence at various American universities. As such, he and his position have become a kind of national institution.

Amherst gave him his first full-time appointment in this capacity in 1916, and for twenty years he continued his association there with frequent leaves to teach at other colleges. In 1919, he established a summer home near South Shaftsbury, Vermont; and in 1920, he helped to found the Bread Loaf School of English in connection with the neighboring Middlebury College. He has continued his relation with this school and with Reginald Cook—its co-founder—up to the present time, lecturing and reading there each summer to writers and teachers from all over America who view him as a sort of *pater familias* for aspiring poets.

While on leave from Amherst, he was poet-in-residence at the University of Michigan (1921-'23), at the New School for Social Research (1931-'35), and for shorter periods at The University of Colorado, at Bowdoin, at Wesleyan, and at the University of California. In 1936, he was appointed Charles Eliot Norton Professor of Poetry at Harvard.

Frost's honors through the intervening years have been many in academic and literary circles. He has received over forty honorary degrees from American universities—more than any other contemporary poet—and he has had a wide following in the academic world of which he has become an active part, setting the popular precedent for poets-in-residence on the American campus today. Besides his American degrees, he has been awarded various poetry prizes and honors: The Levinson Prize, National Institute of Arts and Sciences, Mark Twain Medal, International P.E.N., The Seven Arts, The American Academy of Arts and Letters, The *Jeux Floreaux,* and many others. He has also been awarded the Pulitzer Prize for Poetry more often than any other poet (1924, '31, '37, and '43) and has recently been mentioned in the press as a possible candidate for the next Nobel Prize in Poetry. A group of critics and writers paid him special honor at a dinner on his fiftieth birthday; on his seventy-fifth birthday the United States Senate passed a resolution in his honor offering the "felicitations of the nation which he served so well";[34] and on his eighty-fifth birthday the literary great of America and England honored him with tributes at a commemorative dinner in New York. National literary magazines have published innumerable honoring articles, and a poll of leading critics recently voted his work "most likely to attain the stature of a classic." In 1958, he was named "Consultant in Poetry" to the Library of Congress, the American equivalent to naming him Poet Laureate; and in 1959, a new post was created for him as "Consultant in the Humanities" to the Library of Congress.[35]

He has spent the years of his "retirement" doing what he calls "barding around," visiting college campuses and making lecture appearances. At age eighty, he saved *Poetry* magazine's financial life with a speaking engagement in Chicago. Since his eightieth year, he has made many television performances and a documentary movie, and he never fails to entertain an ever-widening audience with his wit and wisdom in these new media. In his public performances as lecturer today, he still "says" some of his own favorite poems and talks informally about his poetic "prowess and practice." Every now and then he surprises his listeners with some new poem that he tries out before his live audience as a sort of pre-publication test. At the fifty-second annual meeting of the Poetry Society of America, Frost—age eighty-seven—delighted in stumping an international group of distinguished younger poets with quotations from the classics that they failed to recognize.

Besides "barding around" America in recent years, he has been invited to perform abroad in South America, Israel, and the British Isles. His poetry has been taught in literature courses for over forty years at various universities in France, Italy, Canada, England, and Scotland. In 1957, he lectured as a part of the State Department's program for sending artists abroad, read his poetry, and received degrees from Oxford, Cambridge, the Universities of Durham, Manchester, London, and Dublin. Thus the descendant of non-conformist Puritan stock returned triumphantly to the land where he had been completely unknown when he published his first book of poems in London, 1913.[36]

Frost today spends his summers in his retreat near Bread Loaf and his winters in Florida, where he is protected—as much as he will allow himself to be protected—by his devoted companion and secretary, Mrs. Theodore Morrison, who takes much of the burden of being a public figure from his shoulders and allows the freedom he needs for thinking, writing, and "barding."[37] His fame and popularity within the last decade have had phenomenal growth. Over 400,000 copies of his books have been sold, and the American and English public continue to claim him as their poet-sage of the century.[38]

The apex of Frost's career as American bard was reached when President Kennedy invited him to read "The Gift Outright" at the inauguration ceremony in Washington in January, 1961. Frost took his responsibility as representative of the American arts seriously yet whimsically and performed with credit to himself, his colleagues, and his government. On March 26, 1962, his publishers celebrated his eighty-eighth birthday with the publication of his new volume; the President gave him a medal bestowed unanimously by both houses of Congress; and the Secretary of the Interior invited the country's leading citizens to a gala dinner at the Pan-American Union to do him honor.[39]

When a group of Brooklyn clubwomen asked him recently the classic question, "Mr. Frost, how have you found time to be a poet?"—the old eyes twinkled, and Mr. Frost answered them with a characteristic summary of his life:

"Like a sneak, I stole some of it. Like a man, I seized some of it; and I had a little in my tin cup to begin with!"[40]

Chapter Two

Personality and Character

To one who sees and hears Frost, at eighty-eight, read his own poetry, he still gives an impression of great physical strength as he faces an audience; his reserve energy even now seems indicated in every step as he strides across a campus or onto a lecture platform. His stance suggests expectation; his huge head cocked as though always listening beyond the sound, his bright roving eyes alive to more than is actually seen. He is more stooped and slower of speech and reaction than at sixty, but old age has seemed to increase rather than to diminish that aura of vitality that surrounds him. Even if, in these days, he is a little precarious of balance, he still controls a latent force which lies just under the surface of age to be summoned while he is performing. It is only when one sees him off-stage, performance ended, that one realizes, unbelieving, that this is a trembling, tired old man who gives more than he can afford to his listeners.

His features, voice, and personality are familiar today to a wide journalistic and television audience. Though much has been written about the "faunlike" nobility of the youthful Frost's features, today they seem leonine with the shaggy white hair falling informally over a crag-like skull. The well-known voice is still dry and terse as he "says" his poetry with a casual speed that is always surprising. His reading voice-ways are laconic, almost non-commital, as though he wants the poetry to tell all and the personality nothing, though he is meticulous about just the right shading and accent for the "sound of sense." He often gives particular emphasis to certain words of which the casual reader might be unaware until the poetry is heard in Frost's own voice; yet there is somehow an offhand, modest manner about the whole process. He relies little on the printed text but has it before him and leafs through it from time to time with his long fingers selecting old favorites.

His speeches, in the many "asides" that punctuate his readings, are conversational. Always informal, he seems friendly and eager for all human contacts; he encourages with generous response the questions

25

from his audiences and the requests of stage-door autograph hunters, but he is unwilling to sign a blank sheet of paper. There must be some bit of Frost poetry there—some evidence from his own writing that his poetry "has meant something in a life." In conversation he will take time—stopping in midsentence if necessary—to observe some interesting fact in nature, turn it over in his mind, and then finally express it in a few succinct words, or in spiralling sentences as the mood may require.

He is equally at ease in the informality of his Bread Loaf School summer lectures or in the full-dress of a Poetry Arts Club banquet. His approach is the same whether he is under a tree in his own farmyard or under the bright lights of a precisely-timed television program. If his personality shows up to better advantage in one place than in the other, this is not Frost's concern; and indeed his ability to charm any audience into chameleon-like change seems quite independent of place. He recently teased his large television audience on "Meet the Press," with the following warning:

> It takes all sorts of in and outdoor schooling
> To get adapted to my kind of fooling!

Through this "fooling" Poet, the man speaks—as lecturer, teacher, friend, or father.

In his public lectures as well as in his private conversations, his friends class him with the "most interesting talkers of history—Turgenev, Samuel Johnson, Swinburne, and Coleridge."[1] Frost admits that he never plans his lectures or his classes, that he never takes notes or writes his ideas down, feeling that a prepared text for his sort of lecture is disastrous. He says that he prefers to let his philosophies remain rule-of-thumb for fear they will stiffen into intolerant principles, that he has a fear of the abstract and prefers to wait for the real images and objects "of a talker" to come to him without any preliminary organization. He likes to see his audience excited over such active performance, aware of the peril of this sort of loose thinking, yet enjoying it and always succeeding in it.

He admits that he uses his lectures as preparation for the writing of his poems, with many oral trial flights before print:

I'm terrible about my lectures. In my anxiety to keep them as long as possible from becoming a part of my literary life, I leave them rolling around in my head like clouds in the sky. Watch them long enough and you'll see one new form change to another. Though I'm sure they are hardly permissible on the platform, I continue to bring them there with no more apology than to a parlor or classroom. Their chief value to me is what I pick up from them when I cut across them with a poem under emotion. They have been my inner world of raw material, and my instinct has been to keep them raw. That can't long remain their state, however; the day approaches when they

26

will lose their fluidity and in spite of my stirring spoon become crystal. Then one kind of fun will be over. . . Something in me fights off the written word.[2]

As a result, his "lectures" remain today "raw poems," and as such he has best described them himself. Since he is poet first and lecturer-teacher second, he uses both lecture platform and classroom for the practice of his images that eventually make his poems. In a recent television broadcast, he announced frankly that he was going to "rehearse" his very latest "Prayer" for later publication:

> Forgive, O Lord, my little jokes on Thee
> And I'll forgive Thy great big one on me!

His lectures often include a short conversational essay on whatever has seemed significant to him in his current reading and thinking. (In one such performance for *Poetry* magazine, he began by reviewing some of his old high-school translations from Caesar; from one such quotation concerning "glory and honor," he developed what seemed to be a shrewdly organized talk on "pure" versus "functional" poetry including images that re-appeared for several years with changing nuances in subsequent lectures and eventually in poems.[3]) Like any good lecturer, Frost knows which ones will "take" with his audience and is quick to sense rejection or acceptance. His asides to his audience, timed with a professional actor's skill, are sometimes barbed references to particular poets or critics in general who have irritated him in some way. In recent years, some of these comments have a petulance and smugness that force his admirers to wince.

He also has a professional actor's endurance when he travels alone on lecture tours. In his eighty-fifth year, a typical performance day would include luncheon with university officials, an informal class with students in creative writing, dinner with university professors, an evening lecture before two thousand people, and a post-lecture party at which Frost's conversation is the chief entertainment. Even after such an arduous day, he seems reluctant to return to his hotel, making a special effort to speak to each guest individually. He thrives on such activity and attention, admitting openly, "It's what keeps me going, you know. . . . people." (He likes to tell, laughing, how he and his dog make up the only "nightclub" in his Vermont village, defining nightclub as "doing things together after it's midnight"—when they wander down the streets together for their nightly walk.)[4] The easy informality of his "talks" is deceptive, however. True, they seem to meander intuitively as one listens and eagerly follows their many tangents; but the careful listener will note that this professional has had an acute awareness of his every remark upon his audience, an actor's hypnotic and dogmatic command of his listeners, and a precise idea of just where and how his lines have fallen for full effect. At times, he seems almost a *prima donna,* professionally aware of his role and quite delightfully "ham" in his complete enjoyment of it.

The method and range of his thought, in conversation and lecture, have been compared to the dialogues of the peripatetic philosophers. In his lectures, he muses aloud with himself, supplies the answers to his own questions. "Like Emerson, Frost speaks the thought that suggests itself; then like Thoreau, he listens behind himself for his wit."[5] In such meditative moods, Frost sees himself as a political, moral, and social thinker, a simple "bard" with a duty to tell his audience. In each of these areas he constantly points the wisdom of the "Center," and emphasizes the folly of all extremists. His independent "centrism" is as apparent in his philosophic beliefs as in his political and social doctrines. He has consciously avoided formal statements of these attitudes and seems to enjoy the pose of a simple, seeking man who is only an "amateur philosopher." The associative thoughts in his essays, lectures, and letters have frustrated friends and critics who try to organize logically this "wisdom from the heart."

Frost has always been unsympathetic with the efforts of critics who seek to place him in one school or another. In his introduction to *New Hampshire,* he contradicted those early critics who considered him a "mere regionalist":

> Because I wrote my novels in New Hampshire
> Is no proof that I aimed them at New Hampshire.
> I may as well confess myself the author
> Of several books against the world in general.

He has denied the limited birthright of the "literary Yankee tradition" and of the "new transcendentalism." He prefers to be known as a "universalist of the sound of sense, consciously or unconsciously including the tone of voice in sentences that have been my observation and my subject matter."[6] On his eighty-fifth birthday, he answered a critic who celebrated him as "our most famous rural regionalist" with the cryptic remark, "My poetry is both rural and urban. It'd take me several weeks to recognize myself according to him. Actually, I'm a realist."[7] He perfers not to be categorized in *any* geographical or philosophical school. He answers those who accuse him of "spiritual drifting"[8] with the enigmatic couplet which may serve as conclusion to his own philosophy of watchful waiting:

> We dance round in a ring and suppose,
> But the Secret sits in the middle and knows.[9]

With the wisdom of his years and experience, he cautions critics against isolating any poet's philosophic position: "No poet can honestly have one and only one philosophy running through all his work. It's all a matter of mood."[10]

To Frost, lecturing has always been a kind of public teaching; however, his classroom performances please him more than those of the lecture hall. He has been most grateful to those colleges where he has been allowed to teach in his own way and to enjoy his student audiences. With a solemn sense of responsibility, he has said that the future of poetry lies in the hands of teachers in small colleges; and he has been proud to be such a teacher.[11] The experiences in his classes have seemed worth recording to many of his devoted students, some of whom have even published their memoirs. As Frost has progressed from country-school teacher to university lecturer, he has been eulogized by countless students who thank him for their initial introduction to creative writing and reading. One of his earliest students at Pinkerton Academy has described his teaching thus:

He taught with sensitivity, fluent gravity, and friendly lines of countenance. Words and manner were simple, a trace of shyness which attested that simplicity was not an affectation and yet ease. His conversation was dry, sly, ruminating, speculative, critical, as though the growing ends of his feelings still carried him on.[12]

His first official university position at Amherst lists him as a teacher of courses entitled "Judgements" and "English Readings." The pattern that he introduced there for his teaching was much the same as in his original Derry classes—that of "saying poetry, meditating aloud, and bringing fresh associational references from a wide background of non-literary subject-matter. Later when he joined the faculty of a university as poet-in-residence, he established a home close to the campus, gave an occasional talk, received students at his home, and talked to them about literature and life. A colleague who has observed his teaching techniques for over thirty years commends him still as

. . . friendly, sensitive, whimsical, shrewdly philosophic with his students, poised with inner enthusiasm, but never pompous or sententious. He acts as a stimulant and lets the students develop under their own power. Frost told me once that the great moments between student and teacher are rare—perhaps twenty-five by the clock in a lifetime, but how good it is when they come that you were there with the boy![13]

Frost has always maintained that his students must take their own responsibility for learning what literature has to offer, that he is merely a kind of funnel or channel for supplying it. As a college professor in 1921, he lamented the traditional curriculum as a "repository for dead languages, literatures, and ideas" and regretted that some colleges, even then, barred American poetry and contemporary literature from their courses of study. *"Poetry* is not offered at all;"

29

he said; "it is taught like science, language, or grammar, to the discouragement of future poets and readers of poetry." He preferred to teach it as more than just "the rhythmic artistic expression of emotion—rather as an expression of life itself."[14] He has never insisted that poetry be included as an exercise in creative writing and is careful to encourage only those who really *want* to write it; and he warns them that ". . . it's a hard, hard life. Poets come a few a century and wide apart. Number has place in the sciences, not in the arts."[15] As a teacher of literature, he maintains a certain professional self-esteem. Although he respects and has great interest in the natural sciences, he still speaks scornfully of sociology and psychology as "bunko-sciences."

An astute and constant critic of his own profession, he has characterized three kinds of teachers of literature:

1) Men of learning who are strong in cold, historical background and textual scholarship but too modest to insist on what they have in themselves more than learning, too shy to use imagination or wit, too partial to routine.

2) Philosophic expounders of ideologies and tracers of thought movements in literature; too much reform and over philosophizing.

3) Performers in words who are making teaching an adventure, an act of prowess, a sport, a making of things with the mind in the students' presence with the skill one has in danger.

Obviously, he prefers the third variety, and he calls his own method a "doorsy kind of teaching which opens to the outer world."[16]

This "doorsy teaching" method has worked for Frost since his earliest classes to the present day. At a recent university workshop in creative writing where Frost was to speak, young student writers, devotees and cynics alike, came earnestly prepared with professional questions. Frost entered late, jauntily waved his hat at them, smoothed his rumpled hair and bright red tie, stared at them a moment querulously, then said, "Hi!" He rambled a bit about the etymology of his greeting, then said unexpectedly to them, "Talk back!" Before they could recover themselves, he had talked to them about a multitude of things: urban versus rural poetry, the duplicity of good poets, his own "ulteriority complex," his admiration of Odysseus, "bravery" in the arts, Biblical parables, sports, national politics, space travel, his recent conversation with an exterminator he'd met on a diner, the perils of a formal education, etc. Leaving them breathless, he stopped a moment to enjoy their silence, challenged them again—"Come on!" Before they could capture their well-phrased questions, he launched forth again with a series of definitions of education and poetry: "Poetry is that which is lost out of both prose and verse when translated . . ." "All there is to education is hanging around til you catch on . . ." "Your professors will brain-wash you if you don't watch out!" He left them gasping and speechless with his last admonition after his two-hour solo performance: "You've got to snap the whip to make Pegasus prance!"[17]

And yet in spite of his seeming to snap the whip at them, Frost has, through the years, been fondest of all of his youthful student audiences. He knows their zeal and self-consciousness all too well from his own early years. In tribute to his students he entitled a series of talks at Princeton, "The Poet's Next of Kin in a College"; and it is here that he pays his respects to the insights of young people, to their "flashes of light" that later will make up their "constellations of philosophy."[18] He is conscious always of his responsibility as teacher of a sensitive youthful generation even as he demands mature thought and writing from it. He believes that it is best to treat young students with an honesty that is painful when necessary but never sarcastic:

There is danger in undue levity in teasing the young. We must be very careful with our dreamers. They may seem like picketers, or members of the committee on rules for the moment. We shan't mind what they seem if they produce real poetry.[19]

As teacher, Frost has always evidenced the same sincerity of purpose, the same dignity that he cherishes as poet.

Frost's personal relations seem to have been very happy. The fifty years of his marriage to Elinor White were characterized by a mutual devotion and respect and by the intelligent sharing of joy and sorrow. As an uncertain, floundering youth, he had said that all he knew was that, as soon as possible, he "hoped to write a little poem and to marry Elinor" . . .,[20] and the constant sequence of his "love poetry" through his *Complete Poems* shows the depth of this inspiration and devotion. In the dedication of *Mountain Interval,* Frost testifies to the continued serenity of their life together:

To You: who least need reminding that before this interval of the South Branch under the black mountains there was another interval at Plymouth, where we walked in Spring beyond the covered bridge; but that the first interval of all was the old farm, our brook interval. . . .[21]

Throughout the many "invervals," beyond the "further ranges," they always returned to this original source of their happiness together. In the serenely objective poetry that ranges from "Hyla Brook" in the earliest volume through "A Silken Tent" in a late one, Frost continues to speak of the source of their joy: "We love the things we love for what they are. . ." The poetry of this love is over and over marked by a consistent dignity and depth.

Frost has enjoyed his life as father of a large family: a family of six children and many grandchildren and great-grandchildren. His experiences with them have given rise to many a poetic idea. (In a recent lecture he spoke devotedly of a particular image which his modern great-grandson of five years had constructed for him as they visited the Empire State Building together. He tells another story about having to "baby-sit with my grandchildren on either side of the country. First I had to keep one from drowning in the Atlantic; then a little later I had to save one from the Pacific. I bottled a little of each and took it home. Now I call mine the A. and P. farm!")[22] He personally supervised his own children's introduction to literature and the world of nature, although he never insisted on their following either of his own favorite preoccupations. There has been one great sorrow in his family life, he has said: his inability to foresee and prevent the tragic suicide of one son, an invalid whom he described as "a dark spirit always. . ." It is characteristic of Frost's self-control that he should have been able to continue a lecture tour in the midst of this personal tragedy and to have merely alluded in passing to his loss. The poet's own knowledge of the isolation of the human spirit gave him particular understanding of this son for whom he grieved deeply.

He seems to have been equally happy in his personal relations with his Vermont farm neighbors and his university colleagues. He is at home with either group and likes to talk both languages. He still returns each summer to lecture in his "home school" at Bread Loaf and to talk weather and country ballads with the local wiseacres in the village store. As he travels about the country-side at eighty-eight on tour, he is careful to remember his old friends and eager to make new ones. "They won't let me write to you anymore," he says ruefully of his secretaries and guardians, "but you write to me, will you?" There is an old-fashioned courtesy about him as he meets admirers at receptions or talks to airplane or train seat-mates who may never have heard of him. (He recently expressed delight in his anonymity when one such passenger took him for a Texas cattle rancher because of his wide Fedora hat.) An early friend, noting this gregarious versatility of personality, called Frost *homo sapiens* for the multitudes."

Take him for rural New Englander, and he will answer you as a man who played in a boys' gang in San Francisco. Take him for a recluse who has known ferns and rare orchids, and he will surprise you as a reader of the sports page and quote Will Rogers. . . . Assume that he is a poet of experience not much concerned with books, and he will tell you of a story written in ancient Egypt, 5000 B. C. . . . If you infer that he is anti-scientific, you will hear, perhaps, work about the atom. Begin to smile and sigh with him for becoming genial and conservative with friends of wealth and politics, and you will hear a menacing note in his voice and see stern lines around his mouth as he talks of unavenged justice.[24]

One of his oldest friends has recently summarized the personality of Frost today:

He is now an old man . . . with a Yankee shrewdness softened by a life-long indulgence in sensibility and meditation. . . . His talk will range on many subjects, finally on "how to live" . . . He will listen to what you have to say and give it weight and patience; but the part of wisdom for you is to let him do the talking, for he is the best talker I have ever known![25]

A summary of Frost's life in his various *personae* is actually reflected in his poetry, for he has literally *believed* himself into being—from man to Poet. He has shown in many of his prose writings the close relation between his "amateur philosophy of life" and the *raison d'etre* of his poetry.

The myth turns into gospel if the young man believes in himself hard enough and long enough. He will then move from self-belief, through love-belief to art-of-poetry-belief. . . from the foreknowledge of oneness to an actuality of it. This last is literary . . . It is a sort of an investment in the infinite, and it is a good work of art if invested right. All kinds of believing are a partnership in God.[26]

There seems no better word to apply to Frost's view of life—if one must confine oneself to a single term—than "centrist." In an address called "Opposites" which he gave at a testimonial dinner on his twenty-fifth anniversary as a published poet, he concluded that the world is full of opposites: not good versus bad, but qualities that are *all* so good that they destroy each other if they can.

In indifferent times, one quality gets the upper hand, and then its opposite; and the world is torn between extremes of good. The wise man and the good tries to keep in the middle of the road, going his way in a third direction. . . a straight line to certainty.[27]

It is little wonder that "poet-critics" of opposed theories and principles have simultaneously claimed Frost as *their* disciple first and then later accused him of "spiritual drifting." He has been called at once: regionalist and universalist; classicist, romanticist, and realist; individualist and traditionalist; humanist and mystic; skeptic and believer. The basic Frost position seems to have been consistently that of centrist who acknowledges that "both roads" are, after all, very much alike. If he has often seemed to take both roads, he has not lost sight of the point of departure nor the point of eventual meeting; yet he can also respect a friend for whom the divergence "has made all the difference." As for himself, nothing definitive can be announced as yet; ". . . the strong are saying nothing until they see."

In the sequence of the Frost volumes through the years one finds epitomized the poet's own development. Their titles, dedications, and range of poems indicate the series of stages reached in his personal and poetic growth. In its original form, his first book, *A Boy's Will* (1913), had an elaborately annotated table of contents. Each title had a parenthetic gloss describing the author's personal feelings about the poem. Although he later omitted his efforts to explain "the artist as a young man," these titles still indicate his interest in his own emotional development, and one critic has pointed out that in themselves they represent a living metaphor of his personal growth.[28] *North of Boston* (1914) was his first effort to characterize the people with whom he had lived in New England, and the dramatic narratives of this collection reveal great insight into character. They show Frost already deeply aware of the tragedy of a people caught in the decay rather than the flowering of New England. *Mountain Interval* (1916) introduced a new element—the tendency to talk to his readers in conversational, half-critical, half-whimsical tones and to comment openly, as he had not done before (except in narrative), on his attitudes toward life in this interval. He continued this practice in *New Hampshire* (1933) where he frankly begins to explore politics, government, and religion. For *West-Running Brook* (1936) he uses the contradictory image of the first poem as title and expands his former boundaries, obviously leaving the "usual run"—the regional horizon—for the larger world, though still viewing it from a New England vantage point. Here he is more inclined to meditative and philosophic contemplation of the eternal problems of man; his place in the universe, his cosmic struggle with nature, and his precarious yet brave existence at the confluence of the two desperately strong forces. *A Further Range* (1936) makes clear an extension of the political and religious explorations which he had begun in *New Hampshire,* but in a much more didactic manner, using satires, parables, fables, or even direct verse commentaries. In this volume he first directed that some of his poems be "taken doubly" and some "singly." By the time Frost brought out *A Witness Tree* in 1942, his interest in the "further ranges" had diminished, and these poems were concerned with those individual human values that were originally suggested in his first fine lyrics. He has said that the Masques—"Of Reason" (1943) and "Of Mercy" (1946)—held all he knows in their mocking skeptical humor; however, to many critics they seem the work of a garrulous old man who is, consciously or not, playing a joke on his readers. *Steeple Bush,* in 1947, has lyric poems reminiscent of his early style but thematically more like the later poems. When *The Complete Poems of Robert Frost* were published in 1949, their assembled titles and tables of contents indicated this poet's consistent development. Their sequence reveals the transition of his attitude toward his poetry—from youthful subjectivity to mature objectivity productive of his poetry's final purpose.

Since *The Complete Poems,* he has interrupted their finality at intervals with a few pieces in magazines. When he was eighty-five his publishers announced his forthcoming "final" volume to be entitled *The Great Misgiving* and to be brought out "soon." With his usual independence of spirit and meticulous watchful waiting, Frost held off the publication of the new poems for three more years while he "let them lie around to be sure they were just right."[29] And in the end, he changed the title of the volume to a more hopeful symbolism: *In the Clearing.* These last poems represent Frost in his most "bardic" mood and style. At eighty-eight he is consciously committed to telling "all he thought was true" to a world not too fond of advice. He admits that "America Is Hard to See" still, but he continues to add "One More Brevity" as he says farewell in this last volume:

> I opened the door so my last look
> Should be taken outside a house or book
> Before I gave up seeing and slept. . .[29]

He admits that he sees things "begin to close in," and yet he is not willing to give up. After a recent bout with pneumonia, he commented in a rather off-hand way that for the first time in his life he had actually contemplated the idea of death. But he likes to compare himself facetiously with Sophocles, who was still writing at age ninety. He adds jokingly, "I hope to lose my legs before I lose my wits; . . . someday I'll say something foolish!"[30] He hopes to be around to see the new era which he forecast in one of his most recent poems:

> A golden age of Poetry and power
> Of which this noonday's the beginning hour."[31]

When his term ended in 1959, as Poetry Consultant for The Library of Congress, his government as well as his audiences were still unwilling to surrender his services. Upon being offered a three-year assignment as "Honorary Consultant in the Humanities," Frost accepted with a characteristic reply which promised to give him the wide scope he loves for his future:

The Humanities. . . . I more or less arbitrarily take to mean practically everything human that has been brought to book and can be treated in poetry, philosophy, politics, religion, history, and science. Everything, everything. . . .[32]

What modern poet has been more aware of "everything. . ." or more willing to take on sacrifices and challenges as he approaches a century of life still "with miles to go. . ."?

Part Two

His Poetic Philosophy and Practice

"Anything more than the truth would have seemed too weak

. . . .

The fact is the sweetest dream that labor knows."

—"Mowing."

Chapter Three

"Poetry as a Way of Life"

When Robert Frost says that "poetry is a way of life," he is identifying his double role as human being and poet. Critics find it difficult to separate the man from the poet, for he lives as a poet and dedicates his entire existence to the service of his art. For him, the ultimate clarification of life comes through his practice of poetry, and it has become his *raison d'être* By a kind of magic synthesis, exploration and explanation are simultaneous in his adventure; poetry is "all there is to know." Since this relation of poet to poetry is at the heart of the matter, any interpretation of his relationship must begin with Frost's concept of his "belief": how he acts as a poet and how his conduct as a poet is interrelated with the workings of his poetry. One may then consider his experience with the poetic process: its genesis, growth, and evaluation; and finally the analysis of the product itself: the materials from which he makes the poetry—content, form, and mood. The following chapters will attempt to isolate these elements and observe their inter-play.

He is not the theorist of any new approach to poetry; his is the ageless (and often trite) wisdom of the voice of experience. One of the central things about his poetry is that it reflects the experiences of everyday life; its ironies, delicacies, joys, and sorrows. These are not derived from any formal study of philosophy but from life itself. He has the practicality of Arnold, Thoreau, or Hardy; yet he is not as one-sided as they are in his beliefs. His experiences with hard reality have made him basically a teacher through metaphor, and even his simplest couplets depend on this technique for their success. (See "The Secret Sits," "The Span of Life," etc.)

Unlike such of his contemporaries as Ezra Pound and T. S. Eliot, Frost has made no effort to develop a consistent or coherent theory of his poetic art. He has written no single essay on the function of poetry, nor has he written much critical commentary on the practice of other poets which might elucidate his own. It is possible, however, to discover his basic views of art from fragments of his lectures, his readings, his introductions to his own poetry, and his conversations.

Though Ezra Pound was the first poet, as Frost has said, with whom he ever sat down to discuss poetry *per se*,[1] this discussion could hardly have carried agreement of minds. Even in the early days of Imagism, Pound had begun to formulate his revolutionary creed for the "new poetry." Frost retained more conventional patterns and was satisfied with what he called "the old-fashioned way to be new." Though he has plenty of ideas by which a theory of poetry might be constructed, he has expressed these random ideas only in metaphor and has scattered them through his many lectures and his few prose pieces.

The reader of Frost's few essays finds it hard to isolate the poet's principles since he talks of many things at once. Unlike T. S. Eliot, he never explains his own remarks, and his basic principles seem not to have gone through any developing process. His thought may be said to be synthetic rather than analytic; and the analytic reader, not in possession of Frost's mind, will often find himself like the character in "The Armful," who loses the whole by trying momentarily to cling to the part. Since Frost consistently uses metaphor in discussing poetry, his remarks will disappoint those seeking a prose clarification. For them, his explanation of the poetic process does not achieve its end; while for those who already know the poetic experience, his explanation seems redundant.

Such failure to bow to the ordinary analytic approach can understandably create resentment in those who try to interpret his views on poetry. Critics wonder why Frost is not interested in the process of patient explication (though he has been known to complain petulantly that he is not often asked about his *ars poetica*). He continues to talk vaguely of poetry as "a way of life," yet *he* is often unwilling to explain the way in direct statements. For such an explanation the reader must examine the *poetry* within the prose and the *life* within the poetry. He may discover that, when Frost in an essay seems to be dealing with too many things at once, there is a definite coherence if only he can comprehend the metaphors, assemble the random remarks, and disentangle the ambiguities and vagueness of expression. Frost's is a well-filled mind, stocked according to its own laws of coherence, and he has little patience for the hesitant disciple who refuses the hurdles and ignores the detours. His "way of life" is contained not in easy prose parable, but in complex metaphoric poetry. In both the *Collected* and the *Complete Poems*, Frost has consistently used as introduction the artless invitation of "The Pasture"—"You come too." With this he commends to his reader not only a way of *life*, but a way of *poetry*; the two are for him interchangeable.

40

When Robert Frost speaks of poetry as a "way of life," he is consciously avoiding the formality of the word "philosophy." He has never stated any systematic theory for poetry *or* for life, but he has made some epigrammatic statements which seem to summarize and encompass his many metaphoric musings about them. He seems to ask himself constantly, "What does it mean to live as a poet?" He feels a personal duty to answer this question for the reader and to justify with every breath his own recognized high calling. Self-conscious of this duty, aware of his own special gift, he has identified the three "beliefs" which are basic to his poetic life: "self-belief. love-belief, and art-belief."

The person who gets close enough to poetry is going to know more than anybody else knows about the word *belief*. . . I happen to think that those three beliefs are all closely related to the God-belief, and the belief in God is a relationship you enter into with Him to bring about a future.[2]

It is thus the poet's duty to live according to the first three to bring about the fourth. This particular poet's "way of life" is a sequence of these three progressive faiths. He must first know and trust himself and recognize his own human loneliness and isolation in the midst of life. Second, he must know himself as a social being: as lover, friend, teacher, bard. He must be willing to share what he knows with his fellow-man. Finally, he must believe in his creative endowment as artist; he must see himself as form-giver, as hero in his cause. There are the three human conditions of life according to Robert Frost: the bases for what might be called his *religion* for art and life.

Frost is aware of the fact that his "beliefs" are metaphoric and hard to pin down; this is their glory, their pleasure of exploration for him. His poetry contains both the instantaneous flashes of insight that may glitter momentarily in particular lines as well as the constant glow of wisdom that seems reflected from his life itself. It is the balance and tension between the two that make life and poetry keenly interesting for him. Early in life, he was convinced of certain intuited wisdom; his own self-respect kept him throughout the years immune to fads and fancies. The first of his *Complete Poems* is "Into My Own" with the youthful assurance of these lines for any who might try to reform him:

> They would not find me changed from him they knew—
> Only more sure of all I thought was true.[3]

Yet his wisdom did not come from traditional institutional sources, and it was never fitted into any rigid pattern:

> Some may know what they seek in school and church,

And why they seek it there; for what I search
I must go measuring stone walls, perch on perch.[4]

This urge for human independence is at the core of Frost's "self-belief."
He has withstood the attractions of affiliation with both poetic and
philosophic schools throughout a lifetime, confident of his own judge-
ment. Refusing as a youth to be bound by academic disciplines, he
educated himself; refusing as a young poet to be bound by artistic
"schools," he developed his own "sound of sense." Refusing in his
maturity to be categorized by philosophic creeds and scientific theories,
he chooses "something like a star" on which to fix his faith. Over and
over in his poetry he acknowledges the precariousness of his position
as mere human. ("Once by the Pacific" contains enough ominous
warning of cosmic rage to terrorize any space-age reader.) And yet
over and over he reassures his reader that his is the best of all possible
positions: his human in the dark with his "self-belief" *will* continue to
exist. "Since he means to come to a door, he will come to a door,"
for his is a "Willful Homing."

His "self-belief" may lead the man-poet into frequent sorrows, and
Frost would not have him seek any easy escape if he would really know
himself. In his struggle for independence, he will have to yield when
reason conquers emotion, but the majority of Frost's poems celebrate
this very conflict and exult in the evenly-matched elements which he
recognizes within his own spirit:

> Ah, when in the heart of man
> Was it ever less than a treason
> To go with the drift of things,
> To yield with a grace to reason,
> To bow and accept the end
> Of a love or a season.[5]

His is a note of affirmation—realistic affirmation—that accepts a hard
but noble challenge for the human condition. Such poems as "Birches,"
"Directive," and "Neither Out Far Nor In Deep" all indicate the fact
that man seems to seek those things which seem most impossible for
him, those events which are full of risk, danger, and tension. And
Frost's life as a poet has taken its directive from this challenge and
enjoyed its swing "back to earth" whenever the philosophic heights
have made him too dizzy for real understanding.

Second only to his love of human independence in "self-belief" is
his awareness of his human dependence. He knows the precarious condition of the human being in his world and acknowledges that his
very humanity depends upon such a condition of conflict, tension,
and balance. In his title-poem for the volume *West-Running Brook*,
he has used such an image: that of a backward-flowing brook, un-

natural for its particular landscape's terrain. From this image of conflict he develops metaphorically the many supporting tensions which he
finds basic to all human life. He continues to rely on contrast, on
paradox, and on friction to provide images and even meters and
rhythms for all of his poetry because he is convinced that this constant "flow" of life against itself is what keeps him alive as a human.
Contrasts between stability and mobility ("Stars"), between the apparent opposites of illusion and reality ("The Demiurge's Laugh"),
between attack and retreat ("A Drumlin Woodchuck"), between vocation and avocation ("Two Tramps in Mud Time") between free-
will and predestination ("The Lovely Shall Be Choosers") all please
Frost and give him material from life for poetry. The most important
human assets, he says, again and again, are "prowess"—a skill to meet
the barriers of the challenge, and "resourcefulness"—a knowing what
to do when. As as matter of fact, for man, Frost remarks pointedly,
"Resourcefulness is next to understanding." One reads Frost's poetry
with the repeated conviction that for him the ideal of balance, of
graceful compromise, is the secret of the good life. The ebb and flow
of Heraclitus seems to recur over and over as the man-poet Frost
speaks. It is this familiar blend of reluctance and acceptance in their
reconciliation that makes him able to encompass both the tragic and
the comic in life and then translate them into poetry of "divine dis-
content." As this man continues to yearn for permanence and to
recognize his own transience, he becames a truly artistic poet and a
truly philosophic human being.

The self-belief that both independence and dependence sustain leads
inevitably to certain skepticism. It is in his role as strong skeptic—even
as ironist—that Frost sees himself as most human. His paternal inheritance of a rebellious reason and his maternal inheritance of an
emotional mysticism created the potential for such a synthesis in
Frost's personality. His childhood experiences included sorrow and
death; his early maturity brought financial crisis and professional dis-
appontment; and his later years have known wars, depressions, and
man's inhumanity to man. So he has adopted the policy of watchful
waiting and has let it reflect in most of his poetry. The painful recognition of the diminishing of life has been constantly a part of his own
existence, and his first poem reflects this at an early age:

> Ah, I remember me
> How once conspiracy was rife
> Against my life. . .

He learned eventually that out of the very paradox of death-in-life
can grow a strong skepticism and at the same time a strong tendency
to what he calls the "God-belief." He could be sure of one thing:

his own desire for life's full experience even though it contained both the affirmations of emotion and the negations of reason. By steering something of a middle course, he might make a classical adjustment. With a shrewd sense of humor and common sense, he might even enjoy the adjustment and savor the process. Politically, religiously, philosophically, he has been successful in applying the checks and balances of skepticism whenever too rash a judgment of acceptance or denial seemed to tempt him. He has been what he calls "a good Greek" and modulated his "self-belief" in the human situation accordingly.

So the first of Frost's three basic "beliefs"—the "self-belief"—seems to include a triple awareness: his human desire for independence, his human admission of dependence, and his concluding skepticism in the light of the paradoxes he sees about him. The poet moves from this first exploratory stage of "self-belief" to the second stage of "love-belief" as his interest grows wider; he begins to see himself as philosopher for and with others. He concerns himself with communication as a social being, and he begins to use his poems—"each one lighting up the other"—to this end.

He progresses from the proud, ironic isolation of his youthful "self-belief" to the next philosophic sequence that he calls the "love-belief." It is here that he recognizes his position as "lover" in society and feels the obligation to communicate what he has learned in the earlier stage. Once again, the poet-philosopher uses his art to speak for his love of life and to reflect his life in his poetry. It has long been Frost's theory that his poems are "only as good as they are dramatic," and critics find him at his best when his poems "talk back and forth to each other" so that each one becomes a kind of metaphor of his "love-belief" in society. It is this social, dramatic belief in communication that sends Frost across the country still at an advanced age literally "preaching" his doctrine of the poetic life like an evangelist. He has said that the sensible and healthy live "somewhere between self-approval and approval of society."[6] His own "lover's quarrel with the world" urges him to talk and write about his experiences as a living poet. So in many capacities—as father, friend, lover, teacher, lecturer —in the social pattern, he is always bard of this "love-belief" in himself and his poetry, and he is compelled to share this belief: a dramatic necessity.

Everything that is written is as good as it is dramatic; it is drama or nothing. . . It goes deep, and I have always come as near it as I could.[7]

This dramatic necessity of communicating is a real "calling" for him to talk and write what he knows about poetry and life.

Frost has never been satisfied merely to talk and write about poetry; in fact, he has always hesitated to do so. Rather, he believes that he

44

must create and live poetry. The unity of his entire life seems to lie in this synthesis of man-poet. He considers it his duty to bring others to the cause of poetry in a generation when such a cause has seemed peculiarly hopeless. In furthering this cause he has depended as much on his personality to teach the wisdom as on his poetry. His "love-belief" must be shown through the man as well as on the page. He is willing to sell his personality with his poetry if thereby he may support the cause: "It's a part of my career and only the means to an end." Basically a teacher-poet, he has a sound notion of the necessity of communication with his audience, and he acknowledges in the presentation of his poetry the many possible levels that this communication may have. Dedicated to reciprocity in his "love-belief," Frost is not satisfied to sit in seclusion and write. He knows that he is most impressive when he "says" his own works. Confident as a trained actor, he is willing to let the lines speak through him for the cause of poetry generally. Convinced that his is a generation truly in need of poetry, he has tried to persuade the common reader of its value. It is natural for this "common reader" to claim Frost as his own even if he does not adequately understand his poetry. Frost accepts this misfortune as one of the necessary risks of his "love-belief."

Frost's conviction of his dignified position as Poet-in-Society places him in the tradition of other poets with this "love-belief" in communication: the bard, the prophet, the soothsayer. Frost claims for the poet of today the right to aspire to the place of Plato's ideal poet, who sang "not by art but by power divine," though his power as poet banish him from the Republic. While Frost would hesitate to claim divinity as his inspiration, he admits to a certain "madness." (Recently in a discussion of reason versus imagination Frost said to a friend, "Imagination comes first." The friend replied, "Oh no, I'm mad about reasoning!" Frost concluded dryly, "That's what I mean!"[10]) Frost would certainly agree with Plato as to the poet's worth in moving men closer to divinity as their "love-beliefs" make them missionaries for their cause. As a bard, Frost feels the respectability of his own office. However, when twitted about his own spiritual drifting, Frost acknowledges his humanistic middle-of-the-road policy with his poem "For Once, Then, Something." He knows that his own spiritual insight as poet-lover is not a completed, developed faith. Like Pascal he is willing—"once embarked on life"—to wager for things unseen on the basis of those seen. He knows life as he explores it through his poetry, as he imitates it in his poetry, and as he may even shape it by his poetry. He would like to have poetry feed and water the passions today as she did in ancient Greece; he would agree with Plato that she must also "prove her worth as she is useful to the State and to human life."[11]

Frost uses the Platonic image of a driver of a team of horses to symbolize his ideal poet's precarious position as he accepts the responsibility for loving life and writing about it. If the poet's life belies his art, he will not be able to maintain the balance between poetic and personal integrity.

I am unsympathetic with a wide divergence between life and art. . . When has it ever been said that a poet must be a participant of unspeakable experiences? This today is too often the stamp of poetic integrity. . . I see a man riding two horses, one foot on the back of each one. The one horse goes one way, the other a second. His straddle is wide, but before long it's going to hurt him.

Frost recognizes that he may often be hurt in the search for his Platonic ideal; like all "lovers" he may have to compromise with his merely mortal frailties. He has said that he is not "pure Platonist," that he is willing to settle for the beauty of the fact rather than the dream when necessary. "The fact is the sweetest dream that labor knows. . .", but it is up to the poet to make the fact a thing of beauty. Frost, in contemporary civilization, feels the same impulse as Thoreau at Walden to reconcile fact and dream; indeed he finds it just as difficult today to keep the two separated. The "love-belief" compels him to share the wonder of the fact through his poetry and his life, to communicate it dramatically to his audience. The "art-belief," which comes last in the progression of his philosophy, compels him to create the dream in the wonder of his own poetry.

But the dream is not necessarily a utopian condition in society. Frost still values "good fences" between men; "proper zones" between man and God; and only recently he advised political and social reformers of the space-race to stop a while and enjoy a standoff. "Let it stand and deepen its meaning. Let's not be hasty about showdowns."[12] In "Build Soil" he wrote, "Keep off each other and keep each other off." It is the "one-man revolution" that Frost preaches when he admonishes his beloved to accept his way, the individual's own soul-searching that could eventually cleanse all of society. He is thus socially conscious and yet individualistic at the same time in his relations with his family, his students, and his audiences. There is little smugness with this, rather a certain reticence and humility as he wistfully offers his readers a better world because they may love as he has loved. The pride of "The Lesson for Today," "The Code," and "Two Tramps in Mud Time" is dignified and humane. Its beauty lies in its self-sufficiency first, but also in the very human urge to share the love with other understanding spirits who may profit from the experience.

"Love-belief's" compulsion to share observed beauty and truth implies the natural desire to create it—what Frost calls the "art-belief" in the cryptic statement of his philosophy. It is in the capacity of "form-giver" that the poet-artist comes into his own. This is the ultimate in his "way of life" after he has passed through the other two stages, and it is in this capacity that he believes himself closest to "God-belief." Here Frost finds man becoming heroic in his intention to "clarify reality" through his poems; they are his faith in action and his constant concern in the world. He can be sure of his art and take pleasure in its creation, its variety, and its service. Through his own seeking of understanding, he comes finally to the creation of a poem whose fact is his own momentary act of consciousness. This is the god-like artist's greatest moment, and Frost recognizes it as the human form-giver's highest achievement:

When in doubt, there is always form for us to go on with. . . I think it must stroke faith the right way. The artist, the poet, might be expected to be the most aware of such assurance. But it is really everybody's sanity to feel it and live by it. . . The background is hugeness and confusion shading away from where we stand into black and utter chaos; and against the background any small, man-made figure of order and concentration. What pleasanter than that this should be so?[13]

And with such a question the poet reaches his complete aesthetic pleasure in the process of creation out of that confusion. He becomes the God-like figure as he creates a form, however simple; and he gives shape to a faith. He becomes heroic as he lives by it and uses that form for the destiny of others. Such a poet achieves life and faith in action at the moment without worrying about any final understanding of the mysteries of God and the universe. "The fact is the sweetest dream. . .", and it is the visible form of the artifact that the artist has created out of his own virtue for that of others if they will read his knowledgeably. *audience*

In using the fact of his poem to educate and convert, Frost retains a certain quality of his Puritan heritage: non-conformist, self-disciplined, vigorous, pioneering—he would bid his readers to all of these daring tortures by the use of the didactic "fact" of the poem. He invites them to "come too" and to learn what he knows. In the tradition of an Aristotelian or a Hume dialogue, Frost lets the fact of his poem become apparent to his reader through dramatic dialogue, image, and action. Then, as form-giver, he often punctuates for emphasis with a kind of commandment or beatitude. This "fact" of a Frost poem is often found in the line which expresses the poet's proverbial wisdom, and it is always carefully and artistically modulated by the particular qualifications supplied by its context. ("Good fences make good neighbors"; "The best way out is always through.") Frost's "art-belief" in the form-giving poet gives him the right to this kind of teaching of worldly wisdom, though he has not espoused a formal theology. He makes use of the epigrammatic as a kind of litany for his "religion." He seems unique in modern poetry in this use of *sententiae*. Many of his lines are as self-sufficient as a Biblical commandment and as barbed as a witticism from La Roche-foucauld. He summarizes his form-giver's "religious" duty pragmatically when he charges him to create "words that can become deeds."[14]

Having passed through the stages of self-discovery and self-fulfillment in sharing, he now reaches self-expression and justification in the creation of his poems. If he is to be a true artist and form-giver, his wisdom will have been "native to the grain" long before the poet writes the final words of the poem. Frost believes that his "words can become deeds" only after the poet has thoroughly investigated them through actual exploration, and this exploration takes place in the act of creative form-giving. The function of the poetry is thus simultaneous with its process, for it is in the exploration itself that the artist sees and knows. The key to Frost's *ars poetica* seems to be the conclusive statement: "Art serves life by clarifying reality; every form that fulfills its commitment is to the particular degree of its fulfillment an example of prowess in performance."[15] As the form-giving artist progresses from poem to poem in his creativity, the "religious" convictions in his poetry develop. Eventually the combined measurement results in a "clarification of life . . . not necessarily a great clarification, such as sects and cults are founded upon, but in a momentary stay against confusion."[16] Frost seems to suggest that perhaps this is all a modern man may dare ask or expect of his own world. . . "the one world complete in any size/ That I am like to compass, fool or wise."[17]

So it is a kind of "religious" destiny that Frost finally sees for the master poet through this triple development of his belief. This contemporary poet who is engaged in bringing a bard's wisdom to the multitudes has an obligation similar to Emerson's "Sayer," who "stands apart among partial men for the complete man, and apprises us not of his wealth but of the common wealth; he is sovereign and stands on the center."[18] This master-poet, convinced of his responsible place in his society, must therefore shoulder the burden of making his poetry say something significant to his audience. ("Poetry without meaning is still-born," Frost remarks of much modern poetry.[19]) It is because the poet as "Sayer" must hold this position that meaningful poetry is still significant in our time and that poet and poetry must respect and reflect each other. For the purest poetry, Frost believes, wisdom of the heart is always preferable to practiced skills and premeditated philosophies. He scoffs at what he calls the "Scholiasts": "Scholars get their knowledge along projected lines of logic; poets, cavalierly, in the wild, free ways of wit and art."[20] He cautions these "scholiasts" with a casual humor when they retreat to researched referential poetry:

> At least don't use your mind too hard,
> But trust my instinct. . . I'm a bard.[21]

48

"Self-belief, love-belief, art-belief . . . all closely related to the God-belief . . . the relationship you enter into with Him to bring about the future." The final goal of Frost's "way of life" *is* to bring about a future. In an atomic age, he is still not in the least worried about the possibilities for that future; in fact he considers it conceited and disrespectful for modern man to consider himself born to the "worst possible time." Rather it is for Frost the time of greatest challenge, the time for greatest heroic potential. From the careful outline for his character in "A Boy's Will" clear through his eighty-fifth birthday's remarks, Frost has never swerved from courage; it has been a major theme of his life and his poetry. Though he speaks of "God-belief" and faith as the ultimate goals for man, his is a courageous humanism still that will not be swayed by dogma or fear. "Our types of speech coincide with our age-groups; in childhood we prattle; in old age we pray. I'd rather prattle than pray, but maybe that's a sign of second childhood."[23] Certain recent critics have claimed that such remarks result from egotism and senility. This is not the conviction of any careful reader who examines the complete philosophy of Frost insofar as it can be determined from his prose and poetry. Such a statement merely shows his whimsical humility and refreshing sense of humor about any self-righteousness that may threaten to overpower him. He knows that *all* of his poems and prose-statements "talk to each other" to make up the complete metaphor of heroism with which he is mainly concerned:

Courage is the human virtue that counts most—courage to act on limited knowledge and insufficient evidence. That's all any of us have, and so we must have the courage to go ahead and act on the hunch. It's the best we can do.[24]

The limited knowledge and insufficient evidence for any formal philosophy are best summarized, Frost believes, in a good poet's complete works. He has tried to make his own complete poems such a synthesis. He has cautioned that the best poems "talk to each other," that there is no one that can be called the key poem for any honest poet. A cursory examination of all of them and a careful sampling of a representative few will attempt to show their interrelation with his life and with each other in subsequent chapters. "Each poem you read throws light on all the others. Everyone you understand adds real meaning to life."[25]

If a poem offers even a "momentary stay against confusion"—however small and temporary a "clarification of reality"—it has been worthy of the bard who created it; this art-belief in form-giving is for Robert Frost a high religious satisfaction. More than this, he cannot and will not say categorically; he continues to "look out far and in deep" with a shrewd and growing sense that affirmation is somehow stronger in the balance than denial. But he is modest enough to remember that "the strong are saying nothing until they see." This has been *his* "way of life" from the beginning; he continues through his self-belief, love-belief, and art-belief to approach—humbly yet proudly—a God-belief as his life draws to its close. In a recent television show in which he participated, he made some succinct statements regarding the modern battle between scientists and poets. One particular quotation seems to sum up Frost's entire religious attitude of simple faith as he watches the frenzied race for space that characterizes the last decade of his life:

I'm only too willing for science to go her whole length; I'm not afraid of her. Let her go as far as she can to domesticate the moon, my bathroom, or my kitchen. She'll never really touch the "human" in me. Mine is an awe that science can't create. There are only two central things in the world: the germ and the coal. Science can never create these; she can only play with them. There's awe enough for me in that![26]

Chapter Four

Experience: "The Figure a Poem Makes"

Convinced of poetry as his "way of life," Robert Frost has been aware of the process of its creation since his youth; and he has dedicated a lifetime to accepting and fostering it. Totally devoted to his craft and art, he has been willing to sacrifice for it even before he knew much about it in a formal sense. He tells of his boyhood pleasure in recognizing the first aesthetic thrill of two lines whose creation "first set me on my way," and he recalls how he was willing to spend his hard-earned money to buy the poetry of masters who seemed to succeed at the process that he hoped to develop. As a boy in New England, he once went to Boston with only "carfare and eats money" to see the city; instead, he saw a volume of an unknown poet, Francis Thompson. After reading the first few lines of "The Hound of Heaven," he bought the book and walked the twenty-five miles home chanting its music. Such dedication to the art of poetry has made his other labors of teaching, farming, and lecturing only secondary to his real "work"; of them he says, "They are just a secondary means to a primary end."

The primary end for Frost is his labor of love in the experience of making poetry. He has worked in a world and a time apart from poetry; this fact has probably made him more than casually aware of the actual process of "The Figure a Poem Makes." He has spent a great deal of time trying to identify and describe his delight in the experience of "form-giving." This *ars poetica*, always stated in subtle metaphor, seems to include about five main elements: the environment necessary for the creation of poetry, its goal, genesis, growth, and his own evaluation of it. Frost himself laughingly refers to his *dicta* as "contradictions that make sense,"[1] and he realizes that they are all interrelated in a single organic credo.

He has noted that there is no one specific physical locale or *milieu* necessary for the creation of his poetry. The urge to produce is always with him and the process always going on within his head. He makes jokes about poets who think they must have just the right physical environment for creativity. Such a restriction in itself would take away from the "organic quality" of the poem, would mean an "impurity," he believes. He carries the idea and form privately within his head sometimes for months before he ever commits them to paper, and the external environment where this happens makes very little difference to him once the two are ready to be joined. When questioned about the proper place to write poetry, he said, "I was only in Wilkes-Barre, Pennsylvania, once. I had to spend the night there, and I wrote a poem. I think of Wilkes-Barre when I read it, but I hope no one else does! Last place in the world you'd think of—Wilkes-Barre!" He is equally scornful of too-sumptuous working conditions; "If I had a beautiful studio, I'd never paint; I'd have ladies visiting!"[1] And yet he knows the stimulation that a writers' colony can offer through its communication, having been both co-founder and teacher at the Bread Loaf School. His impish disregard for environmental surroundings takes on very much more serious tenor when critics try to classify him in any regionalist school. At his eighty-fifth birthday celebration, Lionel Trilling worried him by calling his poetry "rural, foreign to the urban point of view." Frost considers himself anything but a regionalist or a ruralist, preferring to think of himself as a "realmist."[2]

Although Frost feels that the physical sources and environment of creativity are universal, he is not nearly so diffident about the emotional environment necessary for the process of poetry. For this, certain elements and conditions must prevail. He has stated that literature is a "performance in words," that poetry in particular is the "renewal of words." He is constantly aware of the personal drama of the creation of poetry, and he views the process as an organic thing in itself 'in which process and product are one. As "form-giver," this poet comes to his labor in a particular kind of creative mood for which he is willing to wait and which he is able to identify vaguely as an "emotional wholeness." His fear of self-analysis at this point makes him reluctant to do more than explain this as a "nice kind of summons." He seems to feel that too much examination will somehow destroy its enchantment and its power. He has said that there are three necessary elements for this "performance" that marks the beginning of the process of creativity for him. "The first is an evidence of self-surprise; the second, a cool-morning clarity, the brightness and freshness of growing, expanding things; the third, a ramification with direction."[3] When these are magically present in the right compound, a poem is begun.

Frost takes great satisfaction in the actual creative process of his poetry writing and in his own awareness of his "feelings" as he creates. For him there is an epicurean pleasure in his personal sensations as he forms the "figure a poem makes"; it is as much a physical satisfaction as a spiritual one. He compares his "kinesthetic pleasure" in composition to that of an actor or athlete who delights in performing certain basic skills with precision. And yet there is more in Frost's experience of "poetic prowess" than there is in the athlete's conscious momentary use of his skill or in the actor's well-memorized phrase. Conscious of his ability to arrange words and sounds, he sets the game in motion and then stands off on the sidelines to watch its progress. There are rules for the sequence of this pleasurable game, and he delights to play according to these rules from the moment when he sets down the limitations with the first line until the entire poem takes on nicely-balanced, varied patterns of sound, shape, and sense. He cherishes words and phrases, poring over just the appropriate one in his mind until he is willing to limit it to paper.

Since art is for him a pleasurable prowess, he moves in a kind of graceful euphoria through form to his developing goals, and he views the purity of the outcome as the test of whether or not the artist has really "followed through" with the sportive performance. In spite of a poem's casual beginning, its discipline must be strict for its successful conclusion—strict, and set by the limits of the content first and then by the actual progression of its form. "It should be the pleasure of a poem itself to tell how it can . . . the figure a poem makes." The success of a poem, Frost believes, will be determined by the good sportsmanship with which the author accepts the discipline of his medium:

Anyone who plays a game or a play is that much nearer poetry. If one starts to play with an idea in verse, it must be play all the way through. I like a person who says all his life, "Let's play something!" I dislike a person who says all his life, "Let's play we're something!" To have good art one must play *with* something, words in poetry; materials in art.[4]

And in this spirit of play, Frost wants to "win" with his poetry; in fact, he demonstrates a rather whimsically "religious" fervor for the success of his game: "God seems to me to be something which wants us to win. . ." he remarks casually when questioned about the "philosophy" behind his poetry. For him, the ideal emotional environment for poetry's success must be both sportive and aesthetic.

His offhand statements about his art often seem more intuitive than logical, and they are hard to systematize. He admits that his way of thinking is indirect, and he likes it best that way. It provides him with the constant element of "self-surprise" and provides his readers with "hints only" to his kind of organic process. He has delighted in being a self-styled "synecdochist" of restraint. Aware of varying points of vantage, he is not a poet of all one color or shape, one school or time. In fact, his *Complete Poems* cannot be strictly read as a "chronologically" developing sequence, for many new and old ones are rearranged from the first to the last volumes. Rather they must be read as an organic whole in which Frost hints at many ways of writing and thinking, at the human variability that is any sensitive man's own experience with life. Either "Into My Own" from youth or "Directive" from maturity can represent this "shifty" poet's *ars poetica* as he varies with the moment. He can truly be called a poet of "differences" rather than of "development."[5]

He has never had one "goal" for his poetry, nor has he been willing to be claimed by any one school. He has seemed to save himself from the dangers of two extremes: nothing of content (aestheticism) and nothing except content (didacticism).[6] In the poetry-for-art's-sake-or-poetry-for-thought's-sake controversy that has occupied so many poets and critics, Frost has been consistently unwilling to take sides. He recognizes the problem as an unsolvable mystery, and he will not be caught in one "tendential extreme" or the other. With pleasant banter, he teases his contemporaries about their desperate quest to be new, and he cites arguments for his own central position in this old critical war:

I had it from the youngest lately, "Whereas we once thought literature should be without content, we now know it should be charged with propaganda." Wrong twice, I told him. Wrong twice and of theory prepense. But he returned to the position after a moment out for reassembly. "Surely art can be considered good only if it prompts to action." "How soon?" I asked him.[7]

Frost is unconcerned with the experimentalists who every generation or so would arrive anew at one of the old conclusions by means of some exclusion. While some of his later poems seem to preach in a dogmatic fashion all his own "tendencies," the bulk of the better writing shows the magic of a poetry whose heterogeneous elements are blended by image and metaphor. This mysterious blending is the game for Frost, whether for art *or* thought—a game in which he carefully disciplines himself and his form to catch the spontaneous ideas that come to make up the poetry.

His distinction bewteen "pure" and "impure" poetry does not focus on the relative importance of *dulce* and *utile*. He is not interested in the proponents of purism who contend that disinterestedness is the key to good poetry. He has no quarrel with a compromise such as Coleridge's —that "the immediate end of poetry is pleasure and the ultimate end truth."[8] Frost says it all more simply: "It begins in delight and ends in wisdom." His use of the terms "pure" and "impure" involves another aspect of the problem and one that is directly concerned with the process of the poem. He uses the terminology of Poe's "Poetic Principle," but not his basic meaning. For Poe, the measure of the purity of a poem was determined by the degree of immediate emotional impact (what he called "reasoning imagination,"—"Poetic Intellect"); and its impurity, by the extent of the pressure of other sustaining elements, usually moral or didactic. Frost, however, uses these terms to refer not to "art" and "meaning" or to "delight" and "wisdom," but rather to the relation, in the very genesis of a poem, of content to form. In trying to interpret this relationship and its proper sequence, he moves from an analysis of the function of poetry to an examination of the development of a poem. A poem is "pure" or "impure" genetically. The genesis determines the subsequent relation of its content to its form.

The difference in purity and impurity in poetry rests in whether the poet accepts his commitments and follows through. Poetry is pure by the way in which it starts, that is, by where it takes its source. Impure poetry starts with the whole subject present; pure poetry doesn't begin with the whole subject present. A thing thought through before the artist sets pencil to paper is as distasteful to me as poems written on given subjects for assignment.[9]

So the poetic "way of life" and the poetic experience are actually simultaneously exploratory if each is to be "pure" in Frost's sense.

What is the actual process involved for the poet who accepts the challenge to play the game of pure poetry as Frost conceives it? For him, it is a sequence of emotion, perception, and language. First of all, there is the catching of the "vague mood" which commits the poet; in such a receptive mood the poet happens upon a thought to fit the emotion, then words to fit the thought. This is all an organic kind of process, an unfolding naturally, with no imposition of a fitted pattern or idea.

A poem begins with a lump in the throat; a homesickness or a love-sickness. It is a reaching out toward experience, an effort to find fulfillment. A complete poem is one where an emotion has found its thought and the thought has found the words.[10]

Frost thinks that there is no particular mystery about the actual beginning of a poem; an emotion evokes an idea of its metaphoric image; but which one actually comes first is unimportant to him. He recognizes it when he feels he has "got hold of something." Idea and image may even come together, but form must come later if the poem is to be "pure." Once the poet has seized the idea, the poem must provide the form suitable only to itself. Frost has used a rather glib and somewhat questionable analogy to try to explain his mistrust of starting with form. He recalls that Cellini, preparing the mold for his Perseus, in his eagerness to get the mold hot enough burned up furniture, mold, and all, thus destroying process *and* product. Frost warns that the pre-formed poem is as doomed to failure as was the Florentine artist's work. A more successful analogy is his much-quoted definition of the mood of poetic genesis:

A true poem begins like a true love; each begins with an impulse, a disturbing excitement to which the individual surrenders himself.[11]

In the process of creativity, Frost starts with the feeling of the thing seen and then lets his mind wander over the subject without hurrying it into form or words. He keeps his eye on the subject and carries the seed for the poem in his mind with casual delicacy as though it might wither from too much tending. He calls himself a "furtive worker," and he often waits for years testing various "ways" for the poem in his mind before he commits it to paper. He believes that any successful poem must have a natural, slow growth; its poet must have time to savor the growing kernel. "Most of my poetry," he says, "comes from having gloated over getting the hang of something common enough but queer."[12] His first recognition of "self-surprise" leads him to proceed "from things known to things unknown" as he advised his schoolboys to do with their themes.

The creative moment's "queerness" excites him as a poet trying to describe his own impulse; he calls it the "backward logic of the thing . . . its pure wildness." He is sure that this experience is one common to all thinking men; he does not claim that the poetic impulse is the result of some secret, scarce gift for a limited few. True, the limited few follow it through to poetry; but Frost recognizes the initial tendency in all sensitive people.

Almost everyone should sometime have experienced the fact that a poem is an idea caught fresh in the act of dawning. Also there is such a thing as having a moment . . . and the great thing is to know the moment when you have one.[13]

He has remarked more cryptically in his poetry: "It's knowing what to do with things that counts." Frost insists realistically that this is not a mystical experience of any sort, but an "optimum condition." . . . a good coordination of body, mind, and spirit—when one feels what he describes as a "funny sort of command over words, a nice kind of summons." In such a mood the poetry gets started, and then the poem develops from an "ecstasy at some surprise in the mind." He realizes that this ecstasy is a precarious, razor's-edge condition; that it may easily be lost in overworking the poem, that "felicity can't be fussed into existence."

He gets the clue and is drawn on by what he calls "a gathering metaphor." And at the same time there is the latent urge to rhythm, to form that will fit the idea. Frost is reluctant to decide which is more important or which comes first:

The way a poem goes has been a curious thing in my life; I think the whole begins probably with some sing-song of our race . . . we all begin with Mother Goose. Then the song is as important or more important than the thought. The act of having the thought is what gives quality to the poem. The poem is the act of having the thought. In the poem you don't first know what the thought is, but you know when you've missed it.[14]

In an effort to analyze the process more specifically, he once described how he happened to write "Departmental." He asked himself, "What does it ride on?" and answered, ". . . on a queer feeling, a mood toward something, and then the poem begins to fulfill the mood." So when he watched an ant on the tablecloth, he identified the basic idea already latent in his mind (a satire on bureaucratic society) with the image presented; he caught the "heavy-duty" meter and rhyme that would add to the irony of the idea; and he was able in a responsive mood to go straight ahead with what he calls "triumphal intention with some crosscuts." This eventual triumphal intention is what delights him; watching it form, he recognizes it as the "pure emergence of the poem from the logic of the thing." He concludes:

What is memorable in the writing is the resolved perplexity. Can it be resolved? Aye, there's the leverage! Like a piece of ice on a hot stove, the poem must ride on its own melting.[15]

In Frost's actual composing as in his teaching, he deprecates the use of formal notes. This is not to say that he waits for an inspiration to strike by chance or that he never reworks or revises. He acknowledges filing in his memory hoards of material from experience for freedom of recall . . . "ideas that are like giants throwing shadows ahead of them in the forest." He has traced some of his poems from original ideas stored ten or fifteen years before they were finally "surprised into poetry," erupting from the vast stockpile of his mind at some sudden ignition. (He likes to contrast his own disorganized thoughts with those of his friend Wilfred Gibson, who in the old Georgian days in England used to "scratch every nook and cranny for his daily poem" and then studiously record whatever was left over for the future.) Frost prefers to absorb at leisure, wait through unhurried years for exact expression, "to gloat on the things of this world" until the composing mood comes along. He often "builds soil" still at eighty-eight years old by saying a potential poem over and over to himself or by trying it on many audiences. (Even his most flippant verses about science's race for space were tried in at least a half-dozen different lecture performances and in as many forms before they were finally committed to print in his last volume: "My Cow," "Prayer," etc.) He learns from these experiences about what he calls the "significance of suggestibility,"[16] and he makes revisions and adjustments over and over in his mind. However, he warns young poets not to wait complacently too long: "Practice of an art is more salutary than talk about it. There is nothing more composing than composition."[17]

Once the poet has been "self-surprised" and the poem has been actually begun, its growth becomes a kind of self-discovery through form-giving. Frost has spoken of how the writing of a poem is "like going to the North Pole . . . to see if the adventurer could get back!" And

57

certainly for Frost the growth of the poem is a circular process beginning and ending with his own personal satisfaction. Having made the wager with himself in the first moments of form-giving, the poet must then proceed to prove his way through thought, meter, pattern, image and metaphor. As the poet meditates, the "pure poem" seems to compose itself in a kind of unfolding process from the first clear rational observation through the ramifying ideas and their corresponding metaphors. In trying to explain this process Frost has remarked, "I am free only for my first line. Once I say a line I am committed."[18] Any poet who tries to wrench the poem out of its own organic purity is false to his art, Frost believes. Its own momentum regulates its form, and the poet himself gets an aesthetic satisfaction out of this highly artistic experience. "The best of the poem is when you first make it: the curve that it takes, the shape, the run, the flow; and then you come back to it again and again."[19] The poet's infatuation with the poem steadies into "true love" if the poem succeeds to its own "purity."

No one can hold that the ecstasy should be static and stand still in place. It begins with delight, it inclines to the impulse, it assumes direction with the first line laid down, it runs a course of happy events . . . it ends with its own *dénouement*. It finds its own name as it goes and discovers the best waiting for it in some final phrase at once wise and sad. . . So the poem is somehow believed into existence.[20]

It has been noted that Frost's creative moment seems to resemble the emotional tension of a dramatic recognition scene rather than an "emotion recollected in tranquility."[21] The poet's fresh recognition creates emotional crisis; he is impelled to find release from that crisis; and the resolution is the poem. To the elements of emotion, perception, and language—memory must be added as a catalyst for the compounded poem:

For me the initial delight is in the surprise of remembering something I didn't know I knew. There is the glad recognition long lost, and the rest follows. Step by step, the wonder of unexpected supply keeps growing. The impressions most useful to my purpose seem always those I was unaware of and so made no note of them at the time when they were taken; and the conclusion is come to that like giants we are always hurling experience ahead of us to pave the future with against the day when we may want to strike a line of purpose across it for something.[22]

Frost identifies two such types of recognition; the first comes when the experience in the present inspires an emotional recognition that is more a matter of sensation than perception. Such emotional recognition and tension impel the poet to the physical act of faith without foreseeing the future outcome. The second kind of recognition occurs when the emotional pleasure is derived from a sudden thought which comes into sharp focus through discovery and recognition of a particularly apt correspondence or analogy. The first begins as an emotional response which gradually finds resolution in a thought metaphorically expressed; the second begins with perception of a metaphor, and the rational focus comes later. It is understandable that the poet usually prefers the first kind.

But in the last analysis, the poem does not *really* write itself. Frost knows that as soon as he has accepted the responsibility for his own moment of recognition, he as poet is faced with the tremendous task of choice; testing various meters, metaphors, and images against the purity of the poem itself. It is here that temptation may be greatest; if he fails by allowing his own personal desire to dictate to the poem, he has defiled its chastity; his decisions must be those of the poem's own organic entity, and it is the business of the master-craftsman to know when the line meets the test. From the first moment of recognition, the poet must have a contemplative detachment that allows him to make these decisions knowledgeably.

Frost enjoys the process of choosing his metaphors and meters as something particularly "human." "It all has something to do with how we are made. It is essential to how we think and are as humans. Man likes to bring two things together into one. There is something in all of us of the matchmaker."[23] He feels that he cannot do without this sense of "twoness" in his life or in his poetry, and he jokingly calls it his "ulteriority complex." However, he is delicate and selective with it; it is his practice to let the specific replace the general in the analogy whenever possible. Hence, his love poetry is only infrequently an abstract statement of his emotion; it is more often embodied in an incident, an image, or even a rhythm that carries the emotion subtly within itself. (See "The Silken Tent," "Hyla Brook," "To Earthward.") Frost traces this practice back to his admiration for the classical poetry of the Greeks:

I believe in what the Greeks call synecdoche: the philosophy of the part for the whole . . . touching the hem of the goddess. All that the artist needs is samples. Enough success to know what money is like, enough love to know what women are like! Nature does not complete things; she is chaotic. Man must finish, and he does so by making a garden, building a wall, or writing a poem. That is art.[24]

As the poem condenses in the poet's mind from first vague associative idea through specific metaphor and meter to actual word and phrase, it is the poet's business, Frost says, to choose these final words in two ways: for the sound or tone of the words themselves and also for their symbolic meanings. Put together with this double skill, they will not only give the "sound of sense" but will also transmit a mysterious tone to capture the reader's mind in the poet's own mood. "For a poem is a thought-felt thing, and the felt part of it seems to exist in waves. . ."[25] The thing first "felt" develops as a thing "thought." Frost acknowledges that the artist's problem of keeping it in motion is like "rolling a barrel or taming an untamed horse." He finds his greatest pleasure in the objective realization that he has been "carried off" to the point where his own skill seems interrelated with the natural motion of the poem's growth. With the head holding the heart in harness, Frost is able to admire with naive triumph the successful product of his own creation. This is surely not any smug satisfaction but rather the objective respect of any true artist for his artifact.

The achievement of this objective respect is not an easy or a sudden thing. Frost often waits through many years and versions before his poems are allowed the test of commitment to written line. They lie in his mind until they can pass his private set of rigorous standards. These standards are of three categories. The first are those that he holds for the poem itself: its qualities of sensuous and spiritual insight, of poetic integrity, of honesty to an idea, and of organic symbolism. The second category includes those standards that he holds for the poem's public life: its effect on its readers' lives, its "publicality," its message to its readers, its uniqueness, and its possibilities for interpretation. Finally he insists that it must pass the most rigorous test of all—how he, the poet, feels about it himself.

The first set of qualitative judgments lie within the poem's own structure. It must be constructed so that "every word does something to the other words to form two kinds of peaks—the imaginative kind to the eye and ear and the spiritual kind to the heart and mind." It must be completely accurate in sense impressions if it is to succeed in spiritual insight. (See "Acquainted with the Night," "Desert Places," "Departmental," etc. in Part III.) The poem must have integrity in terms of what Frost calls "purity"; it must have developed without any awkward restrictions imposed by its creator; it must be valid and true to a particular idea, and the metaphors used must carry complete analogy. Fnally, the poem as a whole must be organically committed to a particular idea for which it stands as a "symbol." To explain his particular use of the word "symbol," he has said that the poem "Stopping by Woods on a Snowy Evening" is in itself a commitment to convention— "That's what it's a symbol of."[26] So each poem is "symbolic" in a double sense: it is an argument for an idea and a representation of a particular form.

The second set of tests that Frost makes for his own poetry concerns trial of its public life. Once he has set a poem in motion with all his skill and experience, he knows that it must still achieve something beyond his own control; it must live alone in the "trial by existence" that everything must come to. He is only interested in discussing his poetry when it has meant something to his readers. When he demands—in what may seem sometimes a fatuous manner—quotations from his own poems for autographing, it is his way of saying, "What has my poetry meant to your life? Do you really remember and live it?" It is his test of his own bard's position in society as he explains, "Only when poetry has entered a life will I talk about it."[27] However, he has some qualifications about its public domain. He regrets mere "publicality," and wants to talk to the people who have really understood each poem's "felicity." "A poem goes like a marriage. It starts with a thing as private as love and then moves to the public ceremony of the wedding. It goes from felicity to publicality . . . you have to get away from that 'publicality' back to felicity' again."[28] Instead of mere "publicality" in the press, Frost wants a real *rapport* with the private reader. He is not satisfied with the private associational "new poetry" that speaks only to and for the artist himself; he is no dilettante, and he "writes the poem for keeps." He says that he has never written any "practice pieces," that each of his poems struggles to show its own point of drive, its will to tell. "What we try for in a piece of writing is a little order and true meaning."[29] If the poem does not show order and true meaning to its careful reader, it has not passed Frost's own private test for "felicity." He has occasionally been accused of didacticism, of sometimes wanting to tell his audience too much. Frost scorns the poem that has no message; though he is equally scornful of the poem that has *only* that.

A poem must be a momentary stay against confusion. Each one must clarify something. Making poems encourages a man to see that there is a shapeliness in the world. A poem is an arrest of disorder. . . If you mean to be a man, you must assess the Sphinx. You have to be riddled by it to find something to say.[30]

Having established the necessity of meaning, he then tests the true poem by asking how well it says its particular thing in its own way. It must be unique unto itself. "The height of a poet's performance is to create a poem that can't be retold except in its own words *exactly*." This attitude justifies Frost's skepticism of elaborate explication, his cynicism toward teachers who "translate poems into other and worse English." If a poem succeeds in felicity, it will not need *this* kind of publicality.

And yet he knows that each poem must go beyond its original meaning for the careful and sincere reader. He sometimes finds fun in ridiculing esoteric meanings and motivations attached to his simple lines written in what he calls "auto-intoxication," but he is seriously aware of the fact that the poem speaks beyond him after he has let it go its own way. "I know the first and second meanings for it; whatever else it may have is up to the individual reader."[31] Like Janus, the poem looks both

61

ways—into the poet's private world and out toward the reader's own existence—if it is to succeed. Frost has summed up his entire philosophy about a poem's public life in the following quotation: "A poem is a threshold into a poet's mind as well as a window looking out on reality."[32] The reader will ascribe the particular reality from his own life experience.

The final test is not really of the poem itself, but of the poet's personal and objective feelings about it. Frost is better than most poets about contemplative detachment; this is one of the secrets about his publication intervals—a volume about every seven years.[33] It is also shown in his willingness to mix the poetry of his youth and age indiscriminately after it has mellowed long enough to pass the tests. The poem must be "purified" of personal attachment and subjected to strange environments if it is to stand the test of time. And yet Frost knows that it is not merely time that will make it good or bad. When the poem is new, he applies this candid and patient appraisal to it:

I must have the right kind of feeling about it. I must feel in form when I write it. I must see if I've been too nice to myself. I must set it against the masters of technique and experience to make sure it is all right. It must be interesting, but not interested in itself. I must wait long enough for it. . .[34]

Once it has been waited for and judged good in his own mind, he does not think that "the right reader" will have to wait through years of criticism to recognize its worth. If it has succeeded, the proof will be intrinsic in its initial "discovery" by all sympathetic readers of all time:

It is absurd to think that the only way to tell if a poem is lasting is to wait to see if it lasts. The right reader of a good poem can tell the moment it strikes him that he has an immortal wound . . . that he will never get over it. That is to say, permanence in poetry as in love is perceived instantly. It hasn't to await the test of time. The proof of the poem is not that we have never forgotten it, but that we knew at sight that we could never forget it.[35]

Critics have now had nearly a half-century of Frost's publications to assess according to their own standards as well as his; it is interesting to see that the more astute ones have recognized his worth by the very tests which he himself provides.[36] After the celebration of his eighty-fifth birthday, the *New York Times* critic, J. Donald Adams, wrote in summary of his complete works:

He is in my estimation, the only living American poet whose work will have a long life outside the anthologies, as well as in them. His poetry forms a corporate, integrated body, sure of itself, independent, meaningful, and accessible to the most sophisticated of intelligences. As one looks over his successive volumes, one sees that they possess a cohesiveness, a holding together of their component parts which rises and maintains itself like an arch in stone.[37]

And yet many critics have been perturbed because they could not arrange the poetic philosophy of Robert Frost into any kind of schematized code. They have been bothered when he says artlessly, "All I know is in my poems," or uttered some enigmatic metaphor to "explain" himself. Frost is mildly amused by their confusion, and he answers them with what may be the most telling remark of all: *"I'm* not confused; I'm just well-mixed."[38]

This organic quality seems to be the key to the best of Frost. The intuitive poet has for fifty years been following *both* of his roads taken poetically and philosophically with determination and dedication. As a practicing artist he has won triple triumph in genres so unrelated that they are not often mastered by a single poet: the personal lyric, the dramatic narrative, and the meditative satire. Unfortunately, one cannot always count on the objectivity of his critical remarks in the elucidation of his poetry; but he has never claimed to be a critic, "only a poet." He does say certain things conclusively. He warns that they may not be new things critically; but *should* they be new things? Perhaps his most novel representation of old truths is his own poetic life's example of the *Gestalt* of his own generation—an organic synthesis of man-Poet. . . "well-mixed." In close association with this synthesis of personality is another of poetry: that of content and form wherein the "purity" of the poetry is achieved. In both he seems peculiarly to represent his time.

Frost's unwillingness to codify his views into a formal *ars poetica* takes nothing away from his position as poet. In his announced pose as actor-athlete of the poetic world, he is surely no more sentimentally inept than are most professionals when asked to talk about their first loves. (He himself has said, "We shall not care what they seem if they can write good poems.") Yet the critics and non-poetic public who wait hopefully for the secret formula will feel somehow cheated when the artist says simply, "Read the poetry." In essence this is what Frost has said. It is obvious that he prefers and deserves to be judged by his poems rather than by his sparse writings about poetry. He has given hints to help the reading "singly or doubly," and he has consistently encouraged the natural reader with the mind open enough to catch the "sound of sense." Clearly he has sought to narrow the gulf between poet and reader, but his self-respect is too great to go more than his half of the way. A similar respect for his reader is shown in his expectation of mutual effort for equal pleasure. "You come too . . ." Any reader who accepts the invitation with sensitivity will see that Frost's poetic principles are truly "contradictions that make sense."

Chapter Five

Content: "A Clarification of Reality"

Since Frost's statements about the philosophy and the experience of his poetry are admittedly not those of a systematic theorist, the best understanding of his credo comes through the actual analysis of his poetry. However, such analysis must be undertaken with caution. Frost declares his irritation with readers "who stand at the end of a poem ready in waiting to catch you by the hands with enthusiasm and drag you off balance over the last punctuation mark into more than you meant to say."[1] His answer to them has always been that of the typical artist: "If I had wanted you to know, I should have told you so in the poem." No true poet likes to add prose to his poem, for he knows that in a sense the poem has written itself completely unless it is merely contrived verse. The poet, like the reader, is eventually his own audience, and he recognizes that his poem has been "lived into" over a period of many years before it was written. When it emerges as an artifact of his hand and mind, he too stands off and surveys it wondering at the years of experience that have at last produced it; perhaps he may even be unable to identify all the fragments from his own sub-conscious. Hence, he can make only random comments in prose to describe philosophy and experience. His *real* poetic principle may be best got at by considering three phases of his product—the poetry itself. These include the content of what he has to say: the "clarification of reality"; the form in which he says it: the "sound of sense"; and the tone with which he says it: the "triumph to be reminded." The three subsequent chapters will deal individually with these three phases of Frost's poetic principle as they are actually observable in a general survey of his poetry. The last three chapters of the book will present more detailed explication of specific poems.

Frost admits that for him there is always a "breathless swing between content and form," but his definition of poetry as "a clarification of reality" implies that his first concern is with meaning. As a poet, his purpose and virtue are to develop insights and wisdom that allow him to recognize and represent the apparent conflicts of life's constructive and destructive forces; to find for these themes appropriate subjects; and to develop them by skillful use of metaphor and symbol. He announces the proper sequence of the poet's duty: "In making a poem, one has no right to think of anything *but* subject matter, and after making it, no right to boast of anything *but* form."[2] Once the poet has conceived the theme of the poem, he must shape its subject matter into appropriate metaphor and symbol. At this point in the process, intuition leaves off and logic takes over:

> It is as if you stood astride an idea that lay on the ground and they cut the cord; the subject gets up under you and you ride it. You adjust yourself to the motion of the thing itself. That is your poem.[3]

An examination of Frost's *Complete Poems* shows that one basic principle is carried through many different themes: this is Frost's favorite idea of conflict or antithesis. Standing off at some "vantage point"— where "two roads diverge," or from some "strategic retreat"—the poet views his world (". . . the one world of any size/ That I am like to compass, fool or wise.") and observes that it is constantly in balance because of tension, that man exists in this precarious, daring state in all of his relationships. So it is from this one general idea of conflict (or at least of contrast and paradox) that Frost creates his poems around a half-dozen specific themes. This fact of tension, of antithesis, is observed in man's place in nature, in his work and play, in his loves and fears, in his faith and reason, in his transience and permanence, and in his isolation and communion. The last of these is the most important and indeed the one that gives overtones to all of his poetry. He has been concerned with these themes throughout his poetic career; they appear in his first volume and his last and in all the genres in which he writes. While these themes are obviously common to all poets, Frost tends to treat of their major rather than their minor aspects in man's world today. He is uninterested in the more obvious details, the less important trivia of the "modern" or the "urban," and prefers to write on man's basic, even primitive, premises and values. He is concerned with "natural laws" and speaks of the total environment of man in even the simplest metaphor.

Man's place in nature is the theme of Frost's first published poem. At the age of fifteen he found his own position as precarious as a butterfly's, and he mourned both in his elegy, "My Butterfly":

> When that was, the soft mist
> Of my regret hung not on all the land,
> And I was glad for thee
> And glad for me, I wist.

> Thou didst not know, who tottered, wandering on high
> That fate had made thee for the pleasure of the wind,
> Nor yet did I.

If man's place is as precarious as that of the delicate and fragile-winged creatures, what is the balance that keeps them both alive against and within the great complex of nature? Some thirty years later, when Frost edited his first published volume, he chose to end it with this early effort and its companion piece "Reluctance," in which the youth grown to manhood still asks the question of his place in nature. He walks through the winter's landscape and finds:

> The heart is still aching to seek
> But the feet question "Whither?"

The later poem is more compact and serenely objective; it avoids archaic language, and the theme is objectified in intrinsic image and action. In the last volume of his *Complete Poems,* Frost stakes his objective claim still on "The Witness Tree" for his own rational survival; he warns of the danger of too great a subjectivity in "Now Close All the Windows" and in "The Vantage Point"; and he acknowledges man's short-sightedness in "Neither Out Far Nor In Deep." Still he returns again and again to his own particular native quality of human emotion, this special qualification of Man in nature's ranks; and he repeats proudly in this last volume's "Closed for Good" the old conclusions of his first book:

> Ah, when in the heart of man
> Was it ever less than a treason
> To go with the drift of things,
> To yield with a grace to reason,
> To bow and accept the end
> Of a love or a season?

Frost finds man set off from the rest of nature because he alone is capable of "the dream"—because he is primarily and solely an ideal-creating being; and it is in this antithetical position against the hard reality of nature that this "man—animal" best exists. If the woodchuck's burrow reflects no dream beyond necessity or the spider's web no design beyond coincidence, then Frost is willing to respect their very artlessness but at the same time to command his brother man to further vision, however presumptuous. Frost's man is not necessarily the "Man" of heroic timber that other poets have created in the romantic tradition. Rather, caught unaware, he is the dignified yet simple natural man, democratic in his sympathy, yet aristocratic in his personal reticence. There is much about him that is reminiscent of the tragic hero; and yet one feels that Frost's natural man does not go down to any sentimental defeat.

Cleanth Brooks has said that the greatest virtue of Frost's portrayal s his man's "dramatic decorum," that he is kept in his place, whether is specific native of New England or as nameless observer of some far and deep ocean." In fact his very "manliness" may even show up in his being a little odd, for Frost prefers to portray the atypical man as the human prototype. He is the poet-man in nature who, as the "Star-Splitter," is willing to burn down his house for insurance money with which to buy a telescope. This is the man whose "Beech Tree" is his proud "Proof of being not unbounded/ Though in a world of doubt surrounded"; the man to whom "The Tuft of Flowers" left by an earlier mower gives confirmation of his place at least beside other human beings. "Sand Dunes" tell him that Nature may not know this man as well as he knows himself:

> She may know cove and cape
> But she does not know mankind
> If by any change of shape
> She hopes to cut off mind. . .;

while "Hardwood Groves" convinces him that his is Man's particular way: "However it is in some other world/ I know that this is the way in ours."

His second theme, man at work and play, is offered in a wide variety of subjects and forms. For Frost, work is really a kind of play in that its accomplishment is its sweetest satisfaction. Here is Frost the realist, rather than Frost the dreamer; and these first two contrasting themes show his willingness to see all sides of his "Man." He accepts his responsibilities early for a labor that he knows will be eternal. The young boy losing his hand in "Out, Out. . ." can know death early as man's finale because he has known human labor early. His dignity and maturity are not a matter of chronological age when he has once accepted the responsibility of labor. This responsibility demands that the job be well done, that a mower realize that "Anything more than the truth would have seemed too weak." Even "Two Tramps in Mud Time" have the moral right to doubt the man-poet who seems to labor all for love, with the labor turned into sheer play for himself rather than profitable work for them. The thresher in "The Code" has the right to walk off the job when his professional skill is doubted. And as for the laboring poet—his work as "Pan with Us" must be just as sincere, just as earnestly pursued with mind as with hand if it is to succeed in its particular time and place. This theme includes the concept of variation: the whimsical independence of "the lone striker," and the determination of the wood-carver who insists on an axe-helve "native to the grain." In this paradoxical world, labor is its own reward only when the producing laborer realizes it as an artist for its beauty *and* its play as well as for its utility; Frost feels it a theme worthy of poetry only when each artist-worker plays the game fairly on both sides. His attitude is reminiscent of the classic question of W. B. Yeats: "How can we know the dancer from the dance?"

Frost's experience with love serves as the theme for much of his poetry, and here again there is the paradox of antithesis and reconciliation to be acknowledged. His is the ability to yearn for spiritual and physical communion or to reject it consciously for necessary loneliness. Love, like humanity and labor, is also shadowed with an inescapable isolation. Frost's "lover's quarrel with the world" has indicated this dual necessity of personal attraction and rejection. But when he returns from his necessary isolation to show his beloved "the measure of the little while that I have been away," it is with a heightened devotion. "Love and a Question" shows the young lover who is jealous of any intrusion that fate may project into his emotional satisfaction. "Storm Fear" shows his intense determination to maintain its peak against all the elements. "Hill Wife" and "Home Burial" illustrate his uncanny knowledge of feminine psychology in a crisis. Finally, "Happiness Makes up in Height for What It Lacks in Length" gives a triumphal expression to love's constant struggle for perfection. It is possible to create an extensive anthology of love poetry covering most of the ramifications of this theme from Frost's *Complete Poems*. His love poems often take the form of dramatic narratives, more poignant that those of a more expository nature. In his experience with love as recorded in his poetry, he says that he has "craved strong sweets" and known the disillusionment thereafter. He recognizes the paradoxical torrent of a backward-flowing brook as a typical symbol for its power through tension; yet he also recognizes its weakness in the very fear of his own stronger "Desert Places." When he speaks of closed windows, falling leaves, minor songs of birds, flickering lights, dark sunsets, deserted houses, abandoned farms, disused graveyards, "his time of dusk"—he is acknowledging the universal lament for love that cannot outlast solitude and fear and isolation no matter how hard it may try. Here is the same initial stuff of acceptance that has always made for the classical treatment of this theme.

Man's reason—with its similar successes and failures— is almost as common a theme as his love in Frost's writing. When he comments poetically on man's use of reason, he means reason as it is used constructively, not destructively; as it has a particular quality in his medium. He believes that prose is for grievance, poetry for grief; he leaves argument to prose and reserves his poetry for spiritual values. Frost "reasons" thus: "Poetry deals with a meaning and truth which may clarify the mingled goodness and badness of life without getting too optimistic over the existence of the one or too pessimistic over the existence of the other."[6]

As love must sometimes resort to solitude, so reason must often give up to common sense. "On the Need of Being Versed in Country Things" and "At Woodward's Gardens" both teach this uncomfortable lesson in different ways: one with a delicate lyricism and the other with broad satire. Frost has used reason to berate science ("Why Wait for Science?"), politics ("A Case for Jefferson"), industry ("The Egg and the Machine"), war-mongers ("U. S. King's X"), scholarship ("Haec Fabula Docet"), and philosophy itself ("The Bearer of Evil Tidings"). He admires man in his thinking pose most of all, but he occasionally finds him most ludicrous in this process ("To a Thinker"). If man must sometimes acknowledge that "resourcefulness is next to understanding," Frost believes that this conclusion itself shows the right use of reason in his quest for truth.

Man's ability to reason seems to Frost to illustrate inevitably his "theory of opposites"—two levels of the same basic good. (He has been accused of following in the path of Emerson's "cheerful Monism," but he calls his own attitude that of a "sound, melancholy dualism."') He suggests the close affiliation of these two levels in his treatment of the minor themes of justice and mercy. There is no "reason" for the untimely death in "Out, Out. . .," and "Provide, Provide" recommends common sense in its most ruthless and pragmatic form. Still there is the ever-questioning Job of the masque who knows that though we disparage reason, ". . . all the while it's what we're most concerned with." Frost comments metaphorically in this regard on his "theory of opposites":

Justice and Mercy stand each other off and the present stands up between them. . . They are like two hands that by first tightening and then loosening the double string between them make the tin buzzer buzz like a little buzz-saw.[8]

Frost would like to "flee to the hills where I don't have to choose," but he is constantly driven to choice. In the face of such decision, he bids his readers bravely to the "one-man revolution, the only revolution that is coming"—that of man's reason. Randall Jarrell suggests that Frost too often seems to abandon reason for common sense, and that such an anticlimactic rejection is beyond either justice or mercy.[9] Though it is neither reasonable nor sensible to throw an egg at a machine or to look out myopically neither far nor deep, this universal man-Poet recognizes his very quality of human frailty and failure as the necessary part of the design of mortal man whose spirit can still transcend his mortal strength. He admits ruefully that it *is* man's treason to yield too often with a grace to reason. The very "fragmentary blue" gives that reason the urge for more as it contemplates the vaster blue of the heavens. Finally, it is a particular pride in this thinking

69

man that reasonably expects a human relationship with his Creator. Frost uses this ideal with an ironic overtone even in some of his most flippant verse to show the "two levels of the same basic good":

> I turned to speak to God
> About the world's despair;
> But to make bad matters worse
> I found God wasn't there.

> God turned to speak to me
> (Don't anybody laugh)
> God found I wasn't there,
> At least not over half.[10]

In spite of Frost's admiration for man's reason, he has written as many poems stressing the values of his faith. In fact, one of his most common poetic ideas is the reasonableness of faith, and his logic here is frequently taken from lessons in nature. The capacity for nature's renewal seems direct evidence for the constant renewal of man's faith in this God with Whom Frost adopts a kind of man-to-Man relationship. The poet accepts the design and pattern that he recognizes in this world as theological prophecy for another. So if decayed leaves are pierced by fresh blooms of the next season, he is willing to take this fact as a signal for faith by implication. Yet with a care that is reminiscent of Hume's Dialogues, he is meticulous never to overstep the boundaries of what he himself can actually comprehend by such a process:

> However it is in some other world
> I know that this is the way in ours.[11]

To be valid for Frost, this faith must never deny or violate the real world. Hence the importance of man's learning well the pattern of the present mortality for the eventual understanding of his immortality; hence the awareness that *this* moment is also eternity. Frost finds his verities in slight things: the tuft of flowers, the dust of snow, the sudden clearing of a storm, the slow, smokeless burning of an old woodpile. He admits that man's own careful precautions to assure his immortality are insufficient. He admonishes his orchards in his winter farewell, "Something has to be left to God," and he knows that man must not forget the fact that "There Are, Roughly, Zones" through whose boundaries even a Job cannot penetrate. In "The Onset" he weighs the evidence for his own positive inclinations toward belief with the world's even-present evidence against it (which he is careful to note in detail). In spite of "Design" and its companion piece, "To a Bird Singing in Its Sleep," with their casual mistrust of even a deterministic universe, he concludes: "Yet all the evidence is on my side."

70

He is careful not to expect anything from God; he reminds us that we must depend on ourselves and on one another, and that we may actually profit from doing without Him on occasion. Such a poem is in the tradition of Hardy's "Plaint to Man" in which God seems profitably left out of the picture—"and visioned help unsought, unknown." Leaning over a well-curb seeking some kind of mystic vision of truth is not sufficient to find "For Once, Then, Something." He is sure that God can give both negative and positive evidence to those who go honestly through life. However, it is ironic that the evidences are often denied the most studious seekers:

> Heaven gives its glimpses only to those
> Not in a position to look too close.[12]

This couplet is given lengthy verification in the portrayal of Job in "The Masque of Reason."

Frost knows too that these glimpses may be of one variety one day and of the opposite another. The positive faith known intuitively "While Sitting by a Bush in Broad Sunlight" may be denied that same night by the sheer distance of "Stars" at cold midnight. This poet wants *his* "Birches" to swing him "*toward* Heaven" and then down, since "earth's the best place for love." In survey, it is significant to note that the bulk of the poems expressing a positive religious faith are those of the older Frost, that the skepticism becomes less sharp as the poet matures. From first to last, however, it is still a poetry that asserts quietly and humbly, "The strong are saying nothing until they see."

The last of the secondary themes concerns Frost's time sense: his awareness of constant flux, of the relation of the here and now to the limits of time. Many of his poems treat of this theme of universal change. In "The Generations of Men" and "Maple," he looks deep for the sources of the present and finds them inextricably interwoven with past and future. He treats the theme metaphorically and almost symbolically in "Black Cottage" and in "The Cocoon," and he probes these complex interrelationships in "Directive." With an epigrammatic simplicity he regretfully concludes: "So dawn goes down to day,/ Nothing gold can stay." In "Carpe Diem" he acknowledges the futility of trying to seize the day:

> But bid life seize the present?
> It lives less in the present
> Than in the future always
> And less in both together
> Than in the past. The present
> Is too much for the senses . . .
> Too present to imagine.

71

Yet with a typical Frostian independence he concludes that he *has* tried to do the impossible, and he doesn't regret it: in his very awareness of failure he has somehow succeeded:

> I could give all to time except—except
> What I myself have held . . .
> And what I would not part with I have kept.

In all these secondary themes there is omnipresent Frost's central thematic preoccupation—man's isolation in the midst of communion. His childhood fantasy of man's retreat remains with him through his last poems: "Closed for Good," "One More Brevity." In spite of his conclusion that "Happiness Makes up in Height for What It Lacks in Length," he is never able to maintain complete happiness merely in company with others. He acknowledges even in satiric fable his similarity to "A Drumlin Woodchuck" when he feels it necessary to retreat to his own burrow. Some critics have characterized this kind of "strategic retreat" as a cowardly escape to neutrality.[14] In the poem "An Old Man's Winter Night" Frost admits that such an isolated personality is "a light to no one but himself"—that perhaps one aged man seems not even *self*-sufficient in his isolation. Yet this same aged man had known even in his youth when he heard "The Sound of the Trees" swaying and beckoning to him:

> I shall set forth for somewhere,
> I shall make the reckless choice
> Someday when they are in voice . . .
> I shall have less to say,
> But I shall be gone.

So Frost, who has all his life been "Acquainted with the Night," who has known the greatest desolation of all in his *own* "Desert Places," finds his best poetic representation of life in the recreation of the paradoxical loneliness and isolation within man himself. This final theme becomes the composite of all the others. Involved in these basic themes, Frost scorns lesser, more obvious ones—or he merely alludes to them in terms of their larger concepts. For instance, he simply pauses to say emphatically as he burns a pile of brushwood like any good farmer, "War is for everyone, for children too. . ." and goes about his quiet labors realizing the inherent tragic similarity between man's smallest and largest failures. So with reform in poetry, he believes that here again the most can be done with the least. He suggests that the didactic reform efforts do not succeed in this medium as well as the more lyric "golden" ones. He observes, "Poetry's great anti-lure has often been to live ungolden with the poor, enduring what the ungolden must endure." He regrets that poets must allow their art to be engrossed in pseudo-social theory. Critics have often worried over his apparently indifferent attitude toward social reform; but his own response through his poetry has been to insert very casual lines that show his real awareness of temporal horror, then to proceed to larger concepts which, if truly comprehended and corrected, will encompass the lesser reforms.

Having identified a worthy theme, Frost proceeds with "watchful waiting" to the next precarious stage of the poetic process. He says that he "lets a theme lie around" in his mind until a proper subject happens along to convey it into poetry. His half-dozen abstract themes have been carried by hundreds of specific subjects and developed by thousands of related metaphors and symbols. Frost is able to make the most insignificant natural fact a vehicle for a complex universal theme.

In the tradition of the metaphysical poets, he waits until he finds images and experiences common in human life but uncommon in poetry; from these subjects he fashions his metaphors. For this purpose he seems to prefer three varieties of subject matter: the simple, small objects of nature; the everyday situations of common man's life; and the personality quirks of common man himself. Ordinary as these subjects seem, he uses in their development not only his practical experience but also his reading of the classics.

Frost's nature subjects, whether astronomical, geological, botanical, or zoological, are as numerous as the flora and fauna of New England itself; but they are in no way restricted to geographical boundaries in their application. His subjects may range from local weather lore to interplanetary astronomy; from "considerable specks" to astrometaphysical bodies; from sand dunes to mountain peaks; from frailest orchises to hardwood groves; from a tiny spider to man himself. In fact, it is often by the use of some simple animal subject that Frost achieves his best perspective on human beings ("Stopping by Woods," "The Bear," "The White-tailed Hornet"). He also takes contrasting subjects from the plant world to illuminate his humanistic themes: "The Wind and the Window Flower" reflects man's inconstancy; while "Putting in the Seed' demands a reverence for all growing life. The woods—lovely, dark, and deep—and the stars above them have been two subjects frequently used as symbols for retreat.[15] Frost's realistic treatment of nature shows him not as an aristocrat writing pastorals but rather as a sophisticated rustic who knows a country world well enough to use it precisely and expertly. He does not treat his rural people and places as conventions, ideals, or types. He lets his characters converse with their own terse simplicity as individauls; he describes his places with careful attention to provincial image and local metaphor. (See "The Witch of Coös" and "The Self-Seeker.")

In addition to the simple subjects of nature, Frost likes to use man's relation to the incidents and situations of nature for his subject matter: a farmer assessing his crops, a family picking blueberries from a hidden hoard, a Christmas-tree owner lamenting the exploitation of his woods, a wood-carver designing an axe-helve, man's use of grindstones, witching wands, telephones, woodpiles, bonfires, stoneboats, telescopes, plows, and many other objects that relate to his daily tasks.

He uses an equally wide dramatis personae: census-takers, astronomers, line-gangs, range-finders, housekeepers, plowmen, mowers, shepherds, factory-workers, poker-players, preachers, children, explorers, politicians, aviators, lettter-carriers, lunatics, tramps, salesmen, drunks, and professors. All are treated with candor, perspective, humor, and sympathy.

Frost's education in the humanities has been so thoroughly assimilated and his knowledge garnered so widely as he has travelled through literature that his learning, showing up somewhat casually in his poems, gives the impression of a kind of dilettantism. But when the poetry is examined closely, it is evident that his deliberately slow and thorough absorption has great depth. He is not an allusive poet in the sense of Eliot or Pound; the reader does not need elaborate glosses or translations of foreign passages. But he does need a broad education in the humanities and in humanity for a proper appreciation.

Frost uses his classical and historical background as subtly as his folklore with the expectation that the literate reader will get the full relevance of both. He creates a political eclogue for the twentieth century in the form of Theocritus or Virgil ("Build Soil"); he uses an Ovidian fable with great dexterity ("The Demiurge's Laugh"); he paints himself as a contemporary Pan and expects his readers to supply the necessary myth ("Pan with Us"). He locates precisely the focus of contemporary religion, science, sociology, and politics in a simple four-line satire entitled with childish delight "U. S. King's X, 1946." In an indirect way he gives great significance to "The Trial by Existence" by the use of an allusion to the asphodel plant, whose classical connotations must be familiar to the reader if the poem is to mean anything. He inserts parenthetically in "From Plane to Plane" the fact that his old character Pike is innocent of Shakespeare or Milton, but it is obvious that his reader must be able to recall line and scene to catch the significance of the particular quotations. Frost is as careful in his use of contemporary locales, names, dates, and events as he is in his references to received learning. He has been known to consult local mail-clerks, legal records, anecdotes, almanacs, diaries, and letters in order to make his references precise in color.

The specific subjects that Frost uses to convey his abstract themes are turned into poetry by his use of metaphor and symbol: "As a means to an end, metaphor is like a prism that refracts the blinding white light of emotion into its components." His is a deceptive simplicity, and because of this, his subtle mastery of metaphor may often be missed by the casual reader who takes him for a forthright poet dealing only in statement of fact. The homeliness of Frost's analogy tends to make the reader feel that he need not read him as closely as Eliot or Stevens. Actually Frost's uses of metaphor are as subtle as those of any living poet; he has a definite technique of metaphor which makes his poems work. It is significant that he has devoted more prose pages and oral discussions to this element of his poetry than to any other.

His "old ways to be new" have been compared to the Emersonian view of poetry in which "the thoughts of the present give new arrangement to thoughts of the past" so that the renewed utterance from the perception is fresh. Emerson called the poet "The Sayer" not only because he was "a namer of beauty" but also because he was "a perceiver and dear lover of the harmonies that are in the soul and in matter—and especially of the correspondences between these and those."[16] For both Emerson and Frost, relationships are the essence of metaphor and poetry; and they have both pondered the question, "Is the meaning in a poem a means to an end or the end itself?" When Frost considers the function of poetry, he thinks of metaphor as that rational act of comparison which brings into focus some analogy to sharpen and clarify the apprehension. "At its best," he says, "the metaphor is more than a help to the poem; it *is* the poem."[17] (In this view he is in agreement with Wallace Stevens' theory of metaphor as expressed in *The Necessary Angel*.) In an essay called "Education by Poetry," Frost identifies in detail the importance of this element:

I do not think anybody ever knows the discreet use of metaphor, his own or other people's, unless he has been properly educated in poetry. Poetry begins in trivial metaphors, pretty metaphors, 'grace metaphors,' and goes on to the profoundest thinking we have. Poetry provides the one permissible way of saying one thing and meaning another. People say 'Why don't you say what you mean?' We never do that, being all of us too much poets. We like to talk in parables and hints and indirections—whether from diffidence or some other instinct. . . Unless you are at home in metaphor, you are not at ease in figurative values . . . But it is the height of all poetic thinking, that attempt to say matter in terms of spirit and spirit in terms of matter.[18]

Though Frost—unwilling to lose the common ground between reader and poet—is opposed to using abstract words and esoteric phrases in metaphors, he has always emphasized the fact that words are never accurate conveyors of ideas and images, and that the tone of voice, contrast, meter, all combine in "the sound of sense" which makes or breaks a metaphor. He warns that analogies and comparisons must always be tested to be sure that they convey the intended relationships, so that the rational process of the true wit will counterbalance the emotional, and thus the metaphor will hold clear through all its ramifications. He realizes that emotion alone may have a startling effect on metaphor: "It moves a word from its old base to a new and so renews the roots of its spirit."[19] So the ladder of the apple-picker, the birch tree for the swinger, or the snowy woods for the traveller provide new extensions metaphorically and metaphysically.

One recent study of four Frost metaphors concludes that a "rational validity is the outstanding quality of his theory of correspondence."[20] His metaphors seem always intelligently perceptive in their comparisons, and they suggest that the emotion involved is frequently that of happy discovery for both writer and reader. In all of his lectures on poetic practice, Frost has discussed the use of metaphor by what he calls "inherent parallels." He believes that all thinking except mathematical and scientific thinking is basically metaphorical, and he even acknowledges the possibility of extended metaphor for these abstract fields. "I have wanted for years to go further and further in making metaphor the whole of thinking. The metaphor whose manage we are best taught in poetry—that is all there is to thinking."[21] His prose writing such as "The Figure a Poem Makes" and "Education by Poetry" are full of such examples of "poetic manage."

Many critics, in trying to categorize his art, have asked how Frost's poetry relates to the older metaphysical school; they have noted that his use of metaphor seems less involved with elaborate conceits than that of the older school and that his relationships are more direct. Most of his poems seem to fix on a moment when the physical fact and the mystery that surrounds it seem to cross. This is the dramatic moment when his poem achieves its full significance metaphysically. "The Silken Tent," "Desert Places," "The Bear," and "West-Running Brook" are some examples of the many poems that achieve this poetic sophistication. In every instance Frost treats his physical themes with the imagination of a poet and with the pragmatic touch of the common-sense man dealing with actual experience—a man with a skeptical wit not bound by dogma or system. The metaphysics of Frost's metaphors is always an attempt "to say matter in terms of spirit and spirit in terms of matter." It is an effort to find tangible, physical facts and intangible spiritual facts that may be paralleled *not* as private inventions of the poet, but rather for whatever common likeness actually exists for any discerning reader to share *with* the poet.

Frost has said that at the center of poetic philosophy stands the conviction that poetry must include stubborn, irreducible facts, but he holds his "theory of metaphor" for what he calls "the pleasure of ulteriority," knowing the risk he assumes of being disregarded for

76

evoking only primary experience. One of his critics has imagined a conversation what might occur between Frost and Eliot as a means of showing their contrasting ideas on metaphor:

Frost: 'This parallel is, and I feel thus and so about it.'
Eliot: 'This is the way I feel, and I shall choose this parallel to express it.'[22]

A survey of Frost's use of metaphor shows wide variation and virtuosity. He may use a single metaphor to contain the entire substance of such a lyric as "The Silken Tent." Here is a complete sonnet in a single sentence and a single metaphor, and as such it is one of his most successful syntheses of form and content. Or in contrast, he may employ several metaphors within a very short space as he does in "The White-Tailed Hornet" where he includes the teachings of Freud, and tenets of progressive education, and even the theory of evolution all in a single short poem's metaphoric implications. In such "packed poems' he seems able to juggle various metaphors more adroitly than most modern poets.

He is equally versatile in his use of the condensed or expanded metaphor, though he seems to prefer the latter. There are those of single ornament using mere words or phrases; there are those of heavier weight in which the entire poem functions as a single organic metaphor to carry an analogy or symbol not stated but suggested. The first variety may be observed in the simple four-line poem "Devotion" in which the simple position "of being shore to ocean" completely satisfies the metaphoric description of love. Another such simple metaphor in "Good Hours" describes the small cottages in a row, "up to their shining eyes in snow." A third example in "Putting in the Seed" pictures the sturdy seedlings "shouldering their way and shedding earth crumbs." In each of these cases the metaphor's success depends on the use of a single word for fulfillment. The more complex expanded metaphors occur in such poems as "A Patch of Old Snow" where grimy newspaper fragments on the old snow represent Frost's sad disgust with "the news" of his world, man-made and dull, as contrasted to the news of nature's world. In "Fire and Ice" Frost carries the metaphoric use of physical heat and cold clear through the poem to describe a series of philosophical extremes. The title metaphor of "West-Running Brook" presents the phenomenon of a stream that runs counter to all the natural world around it; and in the very strength and tension of this wonder, Robert Frost finds the metaphor needed to express his own human condition. In "Wild Grapes" he transfers the image of the child clinging precariously on the branch in search of fruit to that of the poet hanging on in spite of scientists and sociologists:

> I had not learned to let go with the hands
> As still I have not learned to with the heart,
> And have no wish to with the heart—nor need—
> That I can see. The mind is not the heart.

A final example of the expanded metaphor is found in "Two Roads" where he puts the whole weight of the poem on the original single image of the diverging paths—"And that has made all the difference."

Frequently Frost's metaphors use indirection or personification to show the emotional tone of their human poet. Metaphors of comparative incident are broadly used in "The Cow in Apple Time" where the human situation is compared indirectly to the animal. In "Spring Pools" the author speaks directly of the human connotation in his summary metaphor: "Let them think twice before they use their powers" . . . without feeling it necessary to identify the pronouns in the comparison. In "November Guest" the human love of "Sorrow" is known too late, and the personification in the recognition scene heightens the man's poignant and precarious position. "The Lovely Shall Be Choosers" presents the fatal irony of free will described with a kind of Faustian prologue; "Revelation" ponders the metaphoric problem of the poet who too often emulates the "babes that play/ At hide-and-seek" or who even imitates "God afar," whose every metaphor is not clearly apparent to his readers. The well-known "Birches" shows the sort of personalized historical progression that Frost uses as the poem moves back and forth in sequence of metaphor between narration and philosophizing—both "up and down":

> So was I once a swinger of birches.
> And so I dream of going back to be . . .
> May no fate willfully misunderstand me . . .
> That would be good both going and coming back.

Frost's metaphors of emotional indirection are successfully turned in "Bereft"—with "no one left but God," in "Ghost House"—which becomes the "strangely aching heart" of the poet-inhabitant, and in "Once by the Pacific"—where an approaching storm of nature reminds the poet that the rage of human nature is equally devastating. "The Bonfire" and "November" carry Frost's subtle metaphoric indirection against the horror of war.

There has been some just critical censure of particular poems in which the metaphors seem to be spelled out with an overbearing didacticism. Frost has, it is true, in some cases seemed to weaken the structure of the poems by the application of these too-obvious moral tags. In "To a Thinker" he spoils the metaphor of the mind's "rocking chair," rocking without direction, by repeating the refrain— "So back and forth"—until he bores the reader to overemphasize the point. However, the familiar progression at the end of "Birches" (as mentioned above) shows his skillful transfer from old to new analogies as the poem moves metaphorically to its climax. Cleanth Brooks has cited examples of Frost's uneven metaphoric practices and has criticized his use of bold metaphors in light verse as bad taste. In some of these cases, the technique seems to be intentional for shock technique and perhaps can be so justified. There are some poems in which Frost seems to ignore the use of metaphor and symbol quite completely. In such cases he is at his worst; and the reader becomes embarrassed as the poet comes downstage to make philosophic asides directly and explicitly to him.

In survey, the poems of Frost that seem most successful in their use of metaphor are "The Silken Tent," where the single-sentence sonnet is "gathered" into a single metaphor; "To Earthward," in which the lover originally "living on air" in his physical ecstasy becomes the wiser man who longs for "weight and strength"; "For Once Then, Something," in which the man who looks against the sun into the depths of the well wonders if he will eventually find Truth at the bottom; and "Acquainted with the Night," in which isolation becomes personified. The one which seems to be the most complete failure metaphorically is the laborious "Lesson for Today," which completely ignores the possibility of any image, metaphor, or symbol and preaches in rhymed couplets.

Frost's "symbolism" is a subject that calls for particular clarification of terms. Actually his use of "symbol" is much simpler than his use of "metaphor" in the strict sense of the words. But in a more complex and general sense, Frost actually is something of a "symbolist" —not the "Symbolist" of the particular French school historic in literary criticism with its insistence on *vers libre* and the recording of interrelated sensations and perceptions—but rather a "symbolist" for whom the entire poem—not any one of the parts—is a symbol. He has written an essay—used as introduction to the Modern Library edition of his works—entitled "The Constant Symbol," in which he defines his ideas not of symbolic subject matter but of symbolic form. He believes that "the whole poem" as a symbol has been constant in the sense that in all generations poems have been written "regular" with commitments to meter and line. So in every successful poem there will be an all-pervasive single symbol which is the poem itself; its details will comprise its total by its symbolic use of synecdoche in which the partial is used to explain the whole. ("Acquainted with the Night" and "The Armful" are examples of this technique.) Some critics have suggested that the "dark woods" image to which he seems to return is more than metaphor—actually almost a formal symbol in much of his poetry.

In the strict sense of the term, he has said that he is against "traditional symbol," which by its very definition precludes discovery. He resents a kind of consecrated image which trails long associations to which it owes its current emotional power. Such symbols, he says, are apt to have actual meaning secondary to their emotional value and thus be weak in their own right. He is opposed to the idea of "the poet's myth" in which poetic symbols need not necessarily be true ones. He is shy of all symbols except those that come naturally in nature; then he is glad to set them down. Those symbols which he allows must be "images native to the grain" that are inherent and understandable. So "The Axe-Helve" may be said to deal symbolically with the craft of metaphor-making as it is practical for any poet. "Pan with Us" presents as its theme the problem of the poet who is bored and confused by not being able to find any "new symbols" with which to sing; and in such a sterile society as ours, he can only ask plaintively, "Sing, sing? What shall he sing?"

In a recent conversation, Frost whimsically remarked that there was one thing he would like to have seen and written about: "I've always wished we had two moons. To see 'em weaving in the sky. It'd be quite a sky!"[23] His wistful comment reveals the poetic mind's constant search for new symbols "with which to sing."

In spite of what he says, Frost's symbols *do* range from the traditional (in a few occasional poems) to the neometaphysical, from the simple to the complex. The more simple are well represented in "The Literate Farmer and the Planet Venus" where starlight and electric-light are obviously the old and new faiths, or in "The Cocoon" and "The Leaf-Treader" which present renewal of life in traditionally symbolic fashion. The cross, the scales, and the sword in "The Peaceful Shepherd" are all easily recognizable as is the snake in "The Axe-Helve." However, "Blueberries" and "After Apple-Picking" both have elaborately magnified symbolic extensions. In some of his poems his use of color seems to carry a metaphysical symbolism: "snow" and "whiteness" are used again and again for death and escape, as are "night" and "darkness"; "rain" and "grey" recur often as symbols of bleakness of spirit.

Though in contact with *Les Symbolistes* through the early Imagists whom he knew, Frost seems through the years not to have been interested in exploring their particular use of the exotic or private symbol, nor in their exaltation of the metaphysical and the blending of sensations. Yet certain of his poems—"To Be Taken Singly or Doubly"—show more of such an influence than he would probably be willing to admit, however much he teases with the sub-title. Though he would not go as far as the Imagist credo of the image for its own sake, his intention that an entire poem "be taken doubly" as "a constant symbol" hints at such a relationship. (See "A Lone Striker," "A Drumlin Woodchuck," etc.)

80

Any analysis of Frost as metaphorist and symbolist must acknowledge his awareness of his own peril. He knows that an over-use of the same metaphor is an easy way out, as is an over-use of a disconnection. He believes that the "new poetry's" juxtaposition of disparate objects and effects may too often result in diffuseness of the poetry. He resents this *"new* way to be new"; and he knows, after all, that it is an ancient trick. He says slyly:

It has lately been found out that it is harder to make a disconnection than a connection. The universe is not a continuity; it has always been a discontinuity. When you write a poem, your first object ought to be to put something into it that nobody can connect with anything else. When you have done that, you have elation. You used to get your fun out of the *expression* of a poem. The 'new-fashioned way' is to enjoy the *theory* on which it's written![24]

Even Yvor Winters, Frost's bitterest philosophical critic, admits that Frost has achieved "real genius in his handling of metaphor" and grudgingly admits examples in the masques where he thinks Frost's metaphors rival those of Yeats.[25] Frost's own evaluation of the importance of metaphor shows his great respect for this most important element of a poem's content:

Enthusiasm is taken through the prism of the intellect and spread on the screen of color, all the way from hyperbole or overstatement at one end to understatement at the other end. It is a long strip of dark lines and many colors. I would be willing to throw away everything but that: enthusiasm tamed with metaphor.[26]

The frontispiece of his last book represents a restatement of this theory of metaphor: ". . . a demonstration/ That the supreme merit/ Lay in risking spirit/ In substantiation."[27] Its title, *In the Clearing,* seems to suggest a symbol of self-awareness: that of an old man who has come through the dark woods of "ulteriority" with all its unknown conflicts and has survived to "wait to watch the water clear."

In conclusion, it may fairly be said that *The Complete Poems of Robert Frost*—through a heterogeneous collection of themes and subjects—does represent a single "symbol" of one man's mind caught up in the drama of the human heritage. Striving, tense in its own world, the mind of Frost as revealed through the content of his poetry seems a combination of a modern Quixote *and* Panza, glorying in its antithesis of romanticism and realism, admitting "roughly" the "zones" beyond which it cannot go, yet thoroughly savoring its own indigenous environment.

Chapter Six

Form: "The Sound of Sense"

When content has haunted the poet long enough, its elements begin to seek a form in which to exist. They seem somehow to synthesize themselves: theme, subject matter, metaphor, and symbol—and to direct their own form in a process that Frost describes as "casting about for something to take hold of." The mood compels, the idea is picked up in "the gathering metaphor," and the form follows organically and sensitively in the poet's mind. He knows enough not to interfere with its dictation of framework.

Emotion comes in form; it shouldn't have to be squeezed *into* form. You can feel a little system about to make, like crystals forming on water, and then they set.[1]

Once the design is set, Frost is very serious about what he calls the "creative challenge in the encounter of form with spirit" and the necessary commitment on the part of the poet. (He cites Herrick's "Daffodils" as an example of a poet's perfectly fulfilling this obligation to his art. "I always marvelled how the second stanza was just as perfect as the first."[2]) Once the process is in motion and the form has begun to shape the subject matter, Frost likes to objectify his role as poet, to stand off and watch with delight the whole process which to him is the basic motion of natural creation:

The most exciting movement in nature is not progress, advance, but expansion and contraction: the opening and shutting of the eye, the hand, the heart, the mind. . . We explore and adventure for a while and then we draw in to consolidate our gains. This breathless swing is between subject matter and form.[3]

In discussing the history of poetry he has noted that, just as science has made the swing from force to matter and back to force, so the arts have made a change from form to content and back to form. He views this as good yet dangerous, admitting that people who are given too much freedom will always sway between freedom and discipline. "Where would I like to exist? I would like to exist alive and in motion between these two things, swaying a little with my times."[4] The discipline of form over the freedom of subject matter makes the game interesting and worthwhile for him. "When they give up form, they are in danger of giving up the whole thing," he has said of the formless poets of his own generation.[5]

By "form," Frost means a composite: stanzaic pattern; rhythm and rhyme relationships; balance and equilibrium of structure; controlled unbalance; relation of emotion to emotion, thought to thought, image to metaphor, specific to general, trivial to significant, transient to permanent. The mystery, the wonder, the virtue, and the magic of poetry lie in this heterogeneity of elements blended into a single autonomous unit called "form." Frost has answered critics who feel that the world has grown old, the people tired, and the language worn out, with his definition of the poet's duty to form: "The thing art does for life is to strip it to form. It is necessary for the poet who has discovered a new world to find new words and arrangements of them."[6] The sensitive poet will reflect these new forms with a variety of structure, meter, and diction. It is this pattern of form that will make the poem more impressive than the prose it might have been, but it must be careful to be better than that prose. Frost likes to use the analogy of the poem as a box with a set or assortment of sentences that just fit together to fill it, and he describes the process of filling the poem as that of "going a-sentencing, watching them swing into form."[7]

These general prose hints as to Frost's concept of form are made more specific by an examination of the various structural forms which his poetry has taken. In an examination of his *Complete Poems,* one notes that he has used mainly three genres: lyric, dramatic narrative, and satire (a term which is used here to include fable, parable, epigram, poetic essay, sermon, and oration). The lyrics are chiefly in short-lined rhymed stanzaic patterns; the dramatic narratives in variations of blank verse; and the satires range from closed couplets to lengthy experiments in free verse. His first few books represent the best of his poetry in terms of these first two forms and anticipate the major lines of later development in the third.

Frost believes that each genre dictates its own certain "sound of sense"—actually the discipline of its own form. In answer to the perennial question of audiences—"Why do you write poems?" he always answers: "To see if I can make them sound different."[8] His chief method of "making them sound different" is the variation of meter and diction. He himself is aware of the limits of meter:

All that can be done with words is soon told. So also with meters—particularly in our language where there are virtually only two—strict iambic or loose. The ancients with many were still poor if they depended on meters for all tune. . . The possibilities for tune from the old dramatic tones of meaning struck across the rigidity of limited meter are endless.[9]

He claims that this necessary mixture of formal meter and dramatic diction is his secret for his successful "crooked straightness" in poetry that has "the sound of sense."

R. P. T. Coffin was the first critic to be really aware of what Frost was doing in this regard. He compared the Frost techniques to ancient patterns of verse and traced this "renewal of words" in spoken rhythmic patterns from Anglo-Saxon through Langland and Chaucer, the Earl of Surrey and Shakespeare, Milton, and Wordsworth. He called the measurements of Frost's poetry "not feet lines, beat lines"; not the measurable patterns of regular dactyls and anapests, but the run-over lines of "the quick beat of talk."[10] Later critics have continued to remark about Frost's particular metrical facility and have noted that he has handled a greater number of English meters than any other modern poet with the exception of Yeats.[11]

A recent survey of Frost's metrical practice lists the following variety of patterns: blank verse, sonnets, heroic couplets, two-stress verse, three-stress verse, four-stress verse, five-stress verse, and ballad verse. One hundred-thirty-one of his three hundred or more poems are in iambic pentameter of which forty-five are blank verse and forty-six are rhymed stanzas.[12] According to his own distinction between strict and loose iambic already noted, Frost chose the latter for the bulk of his work; he feels that this is the most natural English meter. He has never hesitated to vary his cadence for a desired flexibility or to provide for a variety of beat when he felt that the "sound posturing" of sense made such deviation necessary. He has written many poems in the same meter and tries to make them all sound different by such subtle deviation as seems to fit his subject matter. Variations of blank verse alone include such diverse examples as "For Once, Then, Something," "Death of the Hired Man," and "Build Soil." In the first example, the blank verse is used to encompass long six-or-seven line sentences of monologue that give a stream-of-consciousness effect; in the second, the lines and meter are broken and uneven, full of restrained emotional content of the dialogue; while in the last example, the blank verse has a sing-song regularity that lends a flippancy to the satire.

Frost seeks to reconcile and unify three separate planes of sound: the rigid basic accent of the iambic, strict or loose; the sheer sound of words or phrases as they are pronounced without regard to meaning or context; and the shades of meaning derived by tone of voice as they are spoken in a particular context.[13] All three are considered and utilized in his creation of metrical pattern. Not only are the words themselves and their sound quantity important, but so are their variations by contraction, by placement, and by omission. Carefully sustained exclusions, breaks in line pattern, punctuation by rhythmic pauses, and oral breath patterns are all a part of the poet's premeditation as may be seen in the dozen poems explicated in later chapters. Frost has allowed himself little of the diffuseness of free verse, of which he says scornfully, "We used to say that the beauty of poetry was that its rhythm helped you remember it. Free verse is better; now you even re-make it!"[14]

Through the years, Frost has lamented the urge of poets who constantly seek "new ways to be new." He feels that their lack of form is often merely "an omission of punctuation or a grafting of a healthy tissue onto a dead one for novelty."

The old ways to be new no longer serve. Science has put it into our heads that there must be new ways . . . largely by subtraction or elimination . . . without punctuation, without metric frame on which to measure rhythm. I stay content with the old-fashioned way to be new.[15]

Critics agree that Frost's most effective "old-fashioned way" has been his "sound of sense." This effort has been regarded as his most significant contribution to modern poetry's metrical form, and he has been careful to remain always within the discipline which he set for himself at the outset of his career. The mere creation of sentences in rhythmic order with proper rhyme scheme was not enough, and he assumed for himself the larger responsibility of what he called "dramatic necessity."

A dramatic necessity goes deeper into the nature of a sentence. Sentences are not different enough to hold the attention unless they are dramatic. No ingenuity of varying structure will do. All that can save them is the speaking tone of voice somehow entangled in the words and fastened to the page for the ear of imagination. That is all that can save poetry from sing-song, all that can save prose from itself.[16]

Interested always in the sense of meaning that is communicated in dialogue, he explores its psychology for two planes of meaning: the restricted meaning of denotation whether written or spoken, and the additional meaning of connotation received from a particular tone of voice—the bare monotonic word alone in contrast to its conversational sound in context. He believes that every meaning has a certain "sound picture . . . the particular sound and sense of every meaning which an individual is instinctively familiar with, without being conscious of the exact words."[17] This idea was first elaborated by Frost as conscious theory as early as 1915; he realized even then that it was quietly antipathetic to the Poe-Lanier patterns of musical notation in verse. Just after an editor had refused to publish his second poem because it was "too-little like Lanier," Frost had another rejection on the same score from a professional poet, Richard Hovey, who complained that Frost's poems were written "too much in the way people talk." Frost ignored both criticisms and proceeded to try to make his verses even nearer to the qualities of human speech, and it was for this very quality that his poetry was first commended years later by the master-critic Ezra Pound.

Astute critics soon realized that though Frost's poetry had stanzaic and metrical patterns that were conservative in outward appearance, it was not at all in the mellifluous tradition of nineteenth-century verse. Working thus independently to correct what he considered artificiality, Frost turned back to the beliefs of Wordsworth and Emerson, who had stressed the inherent poetic quality of conversational rhythms close to the soil (It is interesting that Frost found not only philosophic independence but also poetic independence from this master Emerson, whom he lists as one of the four greatest Americans[18]). At the same time, Robert Bridges was talking about "speech rhythms," and the Imagists had found metrical correction in *vers libre* with its flexible cadences. Frost did not feel that Whitman or Imagism was as near to his idea as was the advice given in *Monadnoc,* which long before had singled out the speech of New Hampshire men as worthy guides. Emerson did not always practice what he preached in his own poetry, but Frost was willing to try to follow his advice closely. He took for his motto the following Emersonian passage:

> Yet will you learn our ancient speech,
> There the masters who can teach.
> For that hearty English root
> Thrives there unvalued underfoot.[19]

This recommendation led him again and again to listen to the language of Wordsworth's "common man," to recall his early fascination with the conversation of one Charley Hall, country philosopher. It was this quality of "man speaking" that led him to admire so much the successful language of the Shakespearean dialogues— ". . . their lean sharp sentences with the give and take, the thread of thought and action quick, not lost in a rage of metaphor and adjective."[20] Frost believed that if his own words and sentences were true enough, his poetry, patterned after Shakespeare's "natural cursive quality," would not need any reading directions; his lines would read themselves. "You hear talk in the next room; you cannot make out the actual words; but you hear the tone of voice, and you have the essential meaning of what is said."[21]

Three chief tones of voice may be distinguished in Frost's "sound of sense": talking, as in "Mending Wall," where the poet converses with his neighbor and his reader; intoning, as in the dignified finale of "Desert Places;" and a combination of talking and intoning, as in "The Mountain." Frost himself says, "I am on the scales between two things—

intoning and talking; I think I bear a little more toward talking."[22] Since an effective sentence for Frost always has a double duty—that of conveying one meaning by word and syntax and another by tone of voice—he tries in all of his poetry to maintain a balance between the formal meter and the informal rhythmic cadence of the speech idiom and tone. The result is a mixture of epigrammatic and conversational style whose overtones and shaded meanings are for him the very stuff of poetry.

Frost's wide variation of meter can be easily observed in any casual survey of his works. The variation of iambic meters alone (in some fifty out of over three-hundred poems) may be briefly noted in the following representative poems from each of his genres: the lyric—"Design," "The Census-Taker," "The Woodpile," "The Old Barn"; the dramatic narrative—"Mending Wall," "Death of the Hired Man," "Home Burial," "Birches"; the satire—"At Woodward's Gardens," "I Once Had a Cow," "And All We Call American," "One More Brevity," "Build Soil," and "Fragmentary Blue." In each of these highly varied poems, the "natural" quality of the iambic meter is used as a persuasive device to enlist the reader's sympathies. He uses the heroic couplet in situations (over thirty) where its compression is needed to give heightened emphasis: in the lyric—"The Tuft of Flowers," "Our Singing Strength," "The Cow in Apple Time"; the dramatic narrative—"Once By the Pacific," "The Armful"; and in the satire—"A Considerable Speck," and "The Bear." His use of the sonnet form (twenty in all) has never been completely traditional, although his earlier ones show more of the Italian form than of the English. His earliest original use of combinations of the two is "Mowing," and he followed this with later metrical experiments in such sonnets as "Hyla Brook" and "Meeting and Passing." This wide variation of form gives many of the sonnets a dramatic tone in spite of their obviously lyric intent. "Design" and "To a Bird Singing in Its Sleep" represent this mixture of tone and form.

Besides sonnets, couplets, and blank verse, Frost uses other variations of five-stress verse; fifty satires and lyrics are outside these disciplined forms, but "Acquainted with the Night" adopts the even more rigid form of the *terza rima* and shows his great dexterity even within these limits. In spite of his wide use of the "natural" pentameter rhythms, Frost does not insist on the exclusion of others. He uses four-stress verse in over sixty poems: "The Secret Sits," "The Plowman," "Devotion," "House Fear," and "Desert Places" all show the wide range here. Tetrameters are used for his dogmatic professional advice on poetic variation entitled "To a Poem," and the satiric meaning is heightened by the beat of the rhythm. Two-stress verse serves him often to represent a high emotional tension with its economy and breathlessness of line: "The Dust of Snow," "The Rabbit Hunter," "I Will Sing You One—O," etc. The single-beat foot of the spondee is used for heavy emphasis in the tragic "Out, Out . . ." and in "The Death of the Hired Man" where the sense of individual lines of crisis demands such emotional variation. (Further discussion of the metrical problems of individual poems will be treated in subsequent chapters with explications from each of the three genres.)

Frost's informal tone is consistently achieved as the rhythms of natural speech cut across formal meters. He accomplishes this by often substituting unexpected anapests for the traditional iambs so that the natural musical cadence changes from declamation or exposition to conversation. "The Trial by Existence" and "Two Tramps in Mud Time" are representative of such combinations:

> The sun was warm, but the wind was chill—
> You know how it is with an April day
> When the sun is out and the wind is still,
> You're one month on to the middle of May.

"The Demiurge's Laugh," "Blueberries," and "The Peaceful Shepherd" show even more elaborate mixtures of tetrameters and trimeters and pentameters to complicate the texture of both meter *and* rhythm. Such combinations are often effective devices for emotional emphasis as in the last sentence of "In Neglect," where Frost resorts to italics to be sure the reader will get the inflection just right, or in the climax of "Meeting and Passing," where the clever use of rhythm and meter assures comprehension of an otherwise muddled sentence:

> Afterward I went past what you had passed
> Before we met and you what I had passed.

Even in Frost's prose essays a reader is often caught up short by the rhythmic pattern of a sentence which necessitates its being read as a poetic line to get the complete meaning or emphasis of the particular beat. A few sentences from his essay "The Figure a Poem Makes" illustrate this necessity of reading them as poetry:

It should be the pleasure of a poem itself to tell how it can. No tears for the writer, no tears for the reader. I tell how there may be a better wildness of logic than of inconsequence. Like a piece of ice on a hot stove, the poem must ride on its own melting.

In some of his earlier experiments one sees the young poet struggling with certain archaisms and awkward contradictions to achieve the pattern he wants. However, he soon surpassed the rhythmic imperfections of "In a Vale," with its forced contractions; "Waiting," with lines that lack whole feet; and "Prayer in Spring," with syntax strained to fit the meter. The more experienced poet omits words like "wist" and "list" and elisions such as "thou'rt" and achieves an extraordinary range of metrical and stanzaic proficiency by a smooth, inconspicuous rhythmic continuity.

A rather brash independence shows sometimes in his choice of words and rhythms not traditionally poetical; in this regard he is certainly in the "modernist" tradition. Readers' sensibilities may often be jarred by the sudden insertion into an otherwise regular line of such surprising words as "Presto!" "deluxe," "career," "altruism," "eolith," etc. Such intrusions sometimes make the form of the poem hard to read fluently. Frost has said that fluency is a thing to fear, a thing less important than idea; and he purposely avoids it. He may even take pride in breaking up the effect of an inevitable cadence with a prosy injection as in "The Last Mowing" ("It's no more men I'm afraid of... I needn't call you by name," etc.). Such use of modulation in the rise and fall of stressed pauses or hurried phrases of the spoken language gives the casual reader trouble until he catches visually the natural intonations which the voice brings to the poem. Noting this necessity for oral interpretation, critics have called Frost "the soft-spoken Browning who does not over-pack his lines to unintelligibility."[23] They have also compared him to Gerard Manley Hopkins, W. C. Williams, and even to E. E. Cummings in an effort to identify this quality. They have discussed his "fine use of colloquial language without self-consciousness" and praised his idiom that belongs "not only to New England but to all of America's vast, easy, loose way of saying things."[24]

Frost has always accepted the responsibilities of rhyme, and his use of it is as variable as his use of meter and rhythm. With rhyme—as with rhythm—his is a scrupulous honesty to the dramatic, emotional situation of his particular stanzaic form. He enjoys the formality of rhymes that are variations on the old sonnet forms: "Spring Pools," "Freedom of Man," "I Could Give All to Time," "There Are Roughly, Zones," and others. But he also indulges in the *in*formality of rhyme for humor's sake in the poems "The Rose Family" and "Brown's Descent." In his rhyming he chooses words that are living and exact, to be recognized and "thought around and around" as the syllables fall on the ear of the reader. (For example, he rhymes the conversational "so's" and "S'pose" with "rose" in his informal satire on Gertrude Stein's famous poem; and he uses the dialect of a New England farmer who calls "oil"—"ile" to rhyme with "mile" in "Brown's Descent"; in "Desert Places" he rhymes "places" with "space is." Frost knows that as poet he is rhyming not just words and phrases but whole sentences that fall and fit together and must go in as unchanged as the words themselves. Caesuras may be moved slightly to fit the sense of the sentence, and beats may fall irregularly by necessary elisions for emotional content; by the same token, local intonations and inflections may slur syllables into rhyme that is recognizable only to man speaking and reading with the "sound of sense." Examples of such irregularity of rhyme are most obvious in dramatic narratives such as "Death of the Hired Man" and "Maple." They also occur frequently in the lyrics and satires: "Reluctance," "To a Young Wretch," and others. Frost calls these deviations "a straight crookedness as much to be desired in a stick as in a line; or a crooked straightness, an absolutely abandoned zig-zag that goes straight to the mark."[25]

His interest in the spoken language has always led Frost toward the dramatic in poetry, and these two elements of rhythm and rhyme give particular assistance to his lively sense of plot and character. Frost has prided himself on being able to handle them so well in dramatic narratives that they "read themselves" very much as do the lines of Shakespeare. He writes of this attempt in "Snow":

I have three characters speaking in one poem, and I was not satisfied with what they said until I got them to speak so true to their own characters that no mistake could be made as to who was speaking. I would never put the names of the speakers in front of what they said.[26]

The only critic who has ever seriously objected to Frost's "conversational" style is Yvor Winters. He resents what he calls "this most careless and formless of all human utterances: spontaneous, unrevised, a limited vocabulary while poetry should be the most difficult and the most revised of all art forms."[27] (This critic has apparently overlooked the fact that there have always been long periods of revision—often as long as thirty years—before Frost's "natural" poetry has been finally allowed to reach the printed page.) From beginning to end, the dramatic diction of man speaking has been the most important element in the framework of meter, rhythm, and rhyme for all of Frost's poetry. He has acknowledged words dramatically "together or apart" as his servants, and he has enjoyed his complete mastery over them.

Once the subject matter has been submitted to a particular form, internal stylistic devices are used to convey exact meaning. In Frost's poetry these are structurally more often a part of the form itself, but they may sometimes be noted as indigenous to the subject matter. They include such lyric and dramatic techniques as onomatopoeia; introductions *in medias res* with flashbacks for necessary backgrounds; parenthetic expressions for editorial comments; parallelisms for balanced emotional effects; allusions to science, history, the classics; subtle references to contemporary events to promote character, mood, plot; double significance of title or sub-title, and sudden juxtaposition of minimum and maxium detail for shock technique. These devices help create the emotional context of the poems both by physical setting and psychological mood.

"Dust of Snow" demonstrates Frost's use of onomatopoeia. The first line—"The way a crow shook down on me"—contrasts the irritation of the glottal-stopped consonants of "crow" and "shook" to the softer sibilants of "dust" and "snow" in the second line and so assists the emotional meaning of the entire poem. In "Out, Out. . ." the buzz-saw actually *has* "snarled and rattled" onomatopoetically in the reader's ear by the time the first line's falling, rushing rhythms suggest the cruel inevitability of the doom of the last line.

In his dramatic monologues, Frost is fond of starting in the middle of things like all good dramatists, and he seeks the exact spot close to the climax for exposing the plot. With the use of this device, he follows the Shakespearean, metaphysical, and Browning tradition. In "The Housekeeper," the tale begins with the simple statement, "I let myself in at the kitchen door," and the whole sad background is injected by fragments of conversation throughout the progress of the poem. "Storm Fear," "Pan with Us," and "Snow" all strike abruptly into the situation. Similarly "A Servant to Servants" starts in the middle of a conversation, and the characters and situations are to be derived from this alone as it reveals the tortured implication of the title.

His titles serve Frost's single or double purpose, as the sub-titles of direction in *A Further Range* and *A Witness Tree* indicate. He warns the reader that they are "To Be Taken Singly" or "Doubly" and suggests "One or Two," "Two or More," to evoke reader response. Thus "Black Cottage" is not only the physical house black with age but also the spiritual soul black with doom; "A Drumlin Woodchuck" is not just an observation on the animal but an observation on man himself in his own strategic contemporary retreat.

Frost may use his wide learning and experience to assemble the exact shade of character he wishes to portray. In "The Self-Seeker," The Broken One, who knows all the proper scientific names for his beloved flowers, teaches them to a sympathetic child, at the expense of a materialistic lawyer whose only concern is the wasting of his valuable time. The permanence of their Latin syllables is juxtaposed against the tiny ticking of his watch. In another poem, the poet refers to *Memento Mori* and expects the reader to know that the motto of the ancient Alcuin is as good for boys who need "The Lesson for Today" as it was for the young Charlemagne. He may allude in another to the Biblical tale of Abishag and David and expect a literate response to the connotation. In a similar fashion, his knowledge of life in the atomic age is carefully used in precise terms to warn man of the race of science with the awful possibility of history's "end deluxe." He asks quizzically, "Why Wait for Science?"

Sudden juxtaposition often provides shock for the reader, exploding from what seems to be simple microscopic detail into a whole universe of macroscopic significance. So "If design govern in a thing so small. . . ." as the fate of a tiny insect, the reader may be sure that Frost is not *only* discussing the precarious fate of the insignificant white spider and his incongruous associates, but that of all mankind as well.

Frost has remarked that the lyric and dramatic qualities of his poems can never really be separated and certainly they are of common intent as they function together:

Everything written is as good as it is dramatic. It need not declare itself in form, but it is dramatic or nothing. A least lyric alone may have a hard time, but it can make a beginning, and lyric will be piled on lyric until all are easily heard or sung or spoken by a person in a scene, in character, in setting.[27]

His early acknowledgment of this "dramatic necessity" shows in his original attempt to arrange his poems in his first volume's publication so that they might indicate to a discerning reader a spiritual and artistic record of his own mental and emotional drama. He half-seriously jotted down explanatory notes to be used as sub-titles to indicate his own attitude as a youthful "tragic hero" in the sequence of his poems:

"Neglect"
(He is scornful of the folk his scorn cannot reach)
"Revelation"
(He resolves to become intelligible, at least to
himself, since there is no help else. . .)

Frost soon gave up this glossing of poems and let them stand alone for dramatic effect when they were collected years later.

Friends who have watched him as teacher and writer say that be began his wisdom with words by "being afraid of them," and that he has maintained this healthy fear throughout his career as poet. He has lectured frequently on the danger of letting words get the upper hand of the poet, on the necessity of choosing *le mot juste,* and not just accepting the beautiful and easy ones. As a modern poet, he knows that their responsibility is frightening when they are left alone, and he knows that great misunderstanding can come through false explication of them. In his Norton lectures at Harvard he has said that he will not go more than half way to make friends with people through the words of his poetry. They must add *their* half in understanding, for poetry belongs to "the people," not to poets and scholars. Hence, there is always in Frost the message of words for those people who read to understand; the Pound-Eliot researched symbol is not for him. He admits that he desires a wide audience, that he is "part orator"; however, he will never step over his half-way mark to become a revivalist.[28] He keeps a well-mended wall poetically.

He achieves this half-way effect by the stylistic use of what Randall Jarrell calls his "minimal case"; he is a poet who uses slight things for his vehicles, but he seems to transfigure the small things of his poetry so that even his couplets refuse to stay slight. In this way, the final twist of "Dives' Dive" enlarges the mundane poker game to universal significance. Critics find this ability to synthesize one of his greatest talents; Randall Jarrell compliments Frost on being ". . . a rare thing, a completely representative poet, not just a brilliant partial poet who does justice to only a portion of reality."[29] Frost's treating of complex ideas by employing common analogies is his means of achieving T. S. Eliot's "objective correlative," but without the use of researched references. His calculations appear to be more instinctive than premeditated.

When Frost feels that there is a danger of staying too remote from his poetry, he frequently enters it by means of a parenthetic phrase or an aside from poet to reader. The tone of many of these asides is such that they seem to fit the character of the "I" writing as well as the "I" speaking or reading. This tendency is maintained from the early "The Demiurge's Laugh" to the late "One More Brevity." ("'Twas too one-sided a dialogue/ And I wasn't sure I was talking dog. . ." or "We know the literary chatter. . .") In such instances he becomes the *confidante* of his audience, and he may even use an aside to tease his readers or to turn the joke on himself. Again, he may be in league with the reader against the stupidities of "the others" in the world. ("You'd never think she said it, but she said it!") He acknowledges, however, that the better way is not to say too much himself but to let the poem convey his determination. "Dust in the Eyes" speaks for him thus:

> If, as they say, some dust thrown in my eyes
> Will keep my talk from getting overwise,
> I'm not the one for putting off the proof.
> Let it be overwhelming, off a roof
> And round a corner, blizzard snow for dust,
> And blind me to a standstill if it must.

H. H. Waggoner finds such reticent admission a particularly "modern touch" in Frost in that it seems to represent our age of defensive gesture and understatement. He suggests that it is even possible that Frost's personality of plain-spoken informality is a stylistic device to express the conviction that "the fact is the sweetest dream that labor knows." "Frost always prefers the horizontal analogy, the low-pressure conversation. This is a part of his defensive retreat from the too-florid poetry of the 19th cenutry."[30]

It must be admitted that in some cases Frost seems not to seek enough indirection in his poetry; sometimes the poems do not control and contain the ideas artistically; in such cases, they fall into a metered, rhymed prose because they carry too-heavy a burden of generalized fact without a "gathering metaphor." Though the good poems far outnumber the bad, no critic of Frost can overlook this weakness which speaks for itself in "The Onset," "The Lesson for Today," and "To a Thinker." These are hardly more than verse essays with little imagery and an abundance of oratory.

Viewed in summary, however, the elements of form in which Frost succeeds so well—his use of a wide variety of stanzaic rhythms, rhymes, and particular stylistic devices—are those that make up his own unique "sound of sense." He applies his own test and finds that his most successful poetry "stands or falls by its truth within convention."[31] If the lay reader may substitute "content" for "truth" and "form" for "convention," he will see the essence of Frost's *ars poetica* and the high degree of interrelationship between these two vital elements.

Chapter Seven

Mood: "The Triumph to Be Reminded"

The elements of content and form in any poetry are held together by mood. It is with this delicate, ephemeral element that the successful poet evokes the greatest reader response, that he achieves what Frost likes to call "the triumph to be reminded." When poet and reader are *en rapport,* it is indeed the reader's triumph to be reminded of the poet's own mood, and the poet's triumph to have evoked it. So the faithful reader comes to identify this poet by certain characteristics of mood: a combination of style and tone that makes up this poet's own particular hallmark.

This composite in Frost represents a fine blend of caution, critical detachment, shrewd appraisal of self and others, diffidence, dry terseness, and laconic indirection. It includes a humor that ranges from flippancy to bitter irony. Finally, it identifies Frost as skeptic and lover. If he seems to say less than he does, this very ability has frequently assisted him in objectifying himself in his poetry's symbolism and compression. This guarded way of saying things, this "cocked-eyebrow" tone is sometimes identified as "Yankee,"[1] but Frost's does not represent any geographical distinction—rather a manner characteristic of any cautious, sophisticated adult.

Frost seems to objectify his own moods by seeing them with certain humor, with wholesomeness, and with impersonality. At best, the tone is mixed, a montage of varying colors of emotion:

The style is the man. Rather say the style is the way a man takes himself; and to be at all charming or even bearable, the way is almost rigidly prescribed. If it is with outer seriousness, it must be with inner humor. Neither one alone without the other will do.[2]

Many of Frost's critics have pointed out that it is in the projection of "tone" that his poems are most successful. Cleanth Brooks, in particular, has pointed out that Frost has a lower pitch of tone and a simpler surface problem than any other modern poet, but that he manages "by a metaphysical extension to establish a metaphysical tone with no apparent idea of literary pretensions."[3] His native ambivalence of tone is usually the result of an ambiguity of feeling. Even in his humor—as in his skepticism and his love—his "theory of opposites" that underlies all the elements of his poetry is apparent. In "The Leaf-Treader" there is a good example of mingled necessity and regret in the man who knows that he must tread the leaves underfoot season after season if he is to survive himself. Though he would like to go with the leaves—yield to his grief or his humor and be overcome completely—the life spirit within him is too strong to succumb completely. So the original emotional tone of the elegiac lament is later inevitably strengthened by blunt humor and reason.

This problem of extremes of mood and tone is of both psychological and artistic importance to Frost as he introduces his paradoxical elements: humor in grief, pleasure in sadness, brightness in darkness. His critics recognize the result as "atmosphere on two separate planes, a careful suspension between tones."[4] The fact of paradox is not only a part of the mood but also of the reason of the poem; and the one thus complements the other in the recognition of the essential limitations of man and his dream.

Unlike Housman, Frost knows that the "massive calm of permanent truth" has its own limitations artistically, and that to be effective it must be relieved frequently by whimsy and humor. This saving sense of humor is a kind of practical guide to salvation for him, and it leads to high levels of serenity. He has said in one of his poems that the way to understanding is partly mirth, and this is his own basis for developing the vital critical attitude that saves him from taking himself too seriously. So he is able to mingle the trivial with the weighty in his poems and to laugh at the serious result.

The range of his humor is noted in the "wide spread of his voiceways"[5] —from the smiling tenderness of the love lyrics to the scornful raillery of the satires. Some of his latest poems are the most flippantly serious of all: "One More Brevity," "Prayer," "I Once Had a Cow." Like his imagery, his dry humor is best when it resides in the basic, organic tone of the entire poem—as in the lengthy "Bearer of Evil Tidings"—and is not just an inflated whimsy or flat statement tacked on as an afterthought. The humor of certain passages in the masques is not integral but rather often awkwardly interjected or appended. In most poems his humor seems most successful when in a kind of teasing vein he seems to be repeating the secret of Plato: "Serious things cannot be understood without laughable things, nor opposites at all without opposites, if a man is really to have intelligence in either."

In all of Frost's humorous poems there is found a critical attitude which does not reflect a chip on the shoulder so much as an objectivity, a look askance at himself and the rest of the world. This effect is achieved in a variety of ways. His most flippant foolery with serious connotation for himself occurs in the narrative of "Ten Mills," "Brown's Descent," "A Considerable Speck," and "Prayer"; while a gentle teasing of the whole human race is carried in the theme of "The Code," "And All We Call American," "The Armful," "Come In," and "I Once Had a Cow." Humor is evident through voiceways and inflections in an oral reading of "The Rose Family," "The Roadside Stand," "To A Thinker," and "To a Young Wretch"; while characterization provides the humor in such poems as "Snow," "Mending Wall," "Black Cottage," and "The Witch of Coös." In these poems there is often a touch of the sinister, the macabre, mixed with the humor. The philosophic extensions of humor to tragedy are best observed in the parallelisms of nature and man found in "Wind and Rain," "After Apple-Picking," and "The Self-Seeker."

Frost often uses this sense of humor as a means of accepting unpleasant reality. In satire and irony he ranges from casual paradox to bitter scorn. "What Fifty Said" provides a simple statement of satiric contrast that evokes its own rhetorical response. In contrast, "The Lovely Shall Be Choosers" is one of his most complex attempts to use paradoxes of nature as the bases for irony. Political satires such as "To a Thinker," "Build Soil," "The Lesson for Today," and "New Hampshire" are apt to become so didactic that they lose the graceful effect of their classical eclogue patterns and descend to mere prose statement. Far better is the satire of the animal fables in which the analogies speak for themselves in such poems as "Departmental," "The Cow in Apple Time," "The Bear," and "The White-Tailed Hornet." Frost's bitterest scorn shoots through the short light verse in which he attacks the frailties of science, scholasticism, politics, economics, and religion with equal disrespect. ("Why Wait for Science?" "Haec Fabula Docet," "The Egg and the Machine," "U. S. King's X, 1946," "Lines Written in Dejection on the Eve of Great Success.") Besides creating these shorter poems of ironic burden, Frost has so tinged some sections of his longer dramatic narratives and lyrics with irony that epigrammatic ironic couplets stand out in the memory apart from the context of the entire poem. ("The best way out is always through"—from "Servant to Servants," or "The fact is the sweetest dream that labor knows"—from "Mowing.")

Frost's attitude toward the whole precarious problem of humor in poetry is metaphorically summarized in this definition: "Humor is a projection that our feelings set up against our reason."[6] When he mocks, it is as much at himself as at others; yet he warns ironically in "Build Soil":

> Don't let the things I say against myself
> Betray you into taking sides against me
> Or it may get you into trouble with me.

The perspective of his humor has been much discussed by critics and friends who recognize its potentialities for both "fire and ice" and who note always its mixed sad-happy mood. His later poems in *A Witness Tree, Steeple Bush,* and *In the Clearing* are the most mocking and ironic in tone, and yet Frost has said recently that he—"being a gambling man"—is willing to stake everything on a better future. "There'll be lots of bangs and whimpers, but we've had them before and no end."[7] He says that he has found (in spite of personal troubles greater than most men are called upon to bear) more things in life to feel good about than not, a philosophy which he summarizes neatly in the poem "Our Hold on the Planet." He says that he is willing to let science go her whole length to-day in domesticating man; that she will never create, but only play with the two centralities: the germ and the coal. "There's awe enough for me in that!" he quips succinctly when asked if he feels pessimistic about modern man's heartless technology. His courage continues to come from the wisdom of men of spirit and of art rather than from the modern scientist's negative or positive wonders.[8]

In a revealing letter to R.P.T. Coffin, he contrasted the mood of his own humor with that of his old friend E. A. Robinson with an interesting distinction:

We two were close akin up to a certain point of thinking. He would have trusted me to go a good way in speaking for him on the art of poetry. We only parted company over the badness of the world. He was cast in the mold of sadness. I am neither optimist nor pessimist. . . If there is a universal un-fitness or unconformity as of a buttoning up so started that every button on the vest is on the wrong buttonhole and has one empty buttonhole at the top and one naked button at the bottom so far apart that they have no hope of getting together, I don't care to decide whether God did this for the fun of it or for the devil of it. The two expressions come to pretty much the same thing poetically.[9]

So what of "Design" and "The Lovely Shall Be Choosers"? They are honest statements of potential distrust in the great scheme of things, but they are balanced—even overbalanced—by the many trusting statements of the power of man's reason and humor to see with humility into these depths: "For Once, Then, Something." If this is "spiritual drifting," then it is certainly more than the casual vacillation of the inexperienced or the terror of the cowardly. Rather, it is the dignified, premeditated reasoning of a man who acknowledges his time and place honestly:

> Grief may have thought it was grief,
> Care may have thought it was care. . .

But actually it is the factual admission that the mere passage of time—irrespective of man's own emotional crises—has always had a great deal to do with wise finality. Frost's poetry implies not merely an admission but an acceptance of the incongruities of experience that make for divided feelings.

In such a somber serenity, Frost stands in the tradition of the greatest classical poets. His own "Desert Places" scare him more than any of the less fatal claims of science; but still equipped with the comic mask, he is able to gaze without any dizziness into the tragic abyss of "quiet desperation" itself when necessary. Contemporary critics admire this comic vision that can even doubt itself—"a reaction to perceived tragedy more to be admired than the literary tears of many of his contemporaries."[10]

A quiet tone of skepticism is inherent in all the elements of Frost's poetry—in theme, metaphor, subject matter, form, and style. His own humility and reticence quietly, wistfully, and hopefully invite the reader to ". . . come too" if he chooses, but any accompanying reader will have to share Frost's clear-eyed skepticism. This quality in him has been compared to Flaubert's horror of *ideés reçues,* and he seems never sure of his own mind's reaction from one flash to another. He is willing to admit this in many of his widely divergent "religious" poems in which he shows his potential faith next to his admitted agnosticism and accepts the fact that such variance is a normal human condition.

Many of his poems assert his lack of assurance from the cosmos as well as from man himself. "Revelation" and "Birches" discuss the relative safety of things known, but "Misgiving" reminds him never to give up the search—inherent in humanity—for the still unknown:

> I only hope when I am free
> As they are free to go in quest
> Of the knowledge beyond the bounds of life
> It may not seem better for me to rest.

Two poems—"On the Need of Being Versed in Country Things" and "A Minor Bird"—relate a little sadly how unromantic the skepticism of practical knowledge can be when one is forced by sheer reality to forsake the myths one has held dear. Yet Frost has never been satisfied with his own response to any systematic philosophy. He has scorned the tenets of all the *isms* that follow in the wake of the evolutionists. ("Design," "On a Bird Singing in Its Sleep," etc.) He has recognized the inability of man to look out very far or deep, and he has heard with horror "The Demiurge's Laugh" behind him when he thought he was chasing it. He has illogically refused "to give up with the heart" when the mind has long let go ("Wild Grapes"), and he would *like* to tell the "Disused Graveyard" that men have stopped dying; but he is too much of a realist to deny fact. He is sure that in man's original creation "The Aim Was Song" even though erring man has never yet found quite the right tune.

Still he has so often himself been allowed "A Passing Glimpse" of the possibility of Paradise that he is unwilling to give up to a completely negativistic conclusion. He says—like his "good Greek out of New England"—that a certain stoicism is best while waiting. "Let what will be, be."

As a result of such a skepticism, his is a kind of rule-of-thumb salvation of happiness made up from a catholicity of experience between the evidences for faith and for doubt; his is the wide centrality of the strong who wait to know, rather than the aimlessness of the truly weak spiritual drifters. He is primarily concerned with man's isolation; he knows that man *must* make the independent quest alone with all the dignity it deserves and with only whatever help may be admitted from a legitimate correspondence. In *The Masque of Mercy* he asserts that "the saddest thing in life is that the best thing in it should be courage." He confesses with his protagonist that, being mere men—

> We both have lacked the courage of the heart
> To overcome the fear within the soul
> And go ahead to any accomplishment.

He knows that this fear within the soul is man's own self-made damnation, this courage of the heart his own constant goal and salvation ("Kit Marlowe taught me how to say my prayers/ Why this is Hell, nor am I out of it!").

Yet this skeptical relativist is willing to make a few indefinite remarks concerning his relation with a deity whom he respects from long experience:

God is that which a man is sure cares, and will save him no matter how many times or how completely he has failed. The belief in God is a relationship you enter into with Him to bring about a future.[11]

It is this relationship that makes the humanism of Frost's poetry. He himself has said that his humanism is "accidental"—the result of his criticism of the "scientism of materialism."[12] Resenting an age that seeks scientific absolutes, he returns again and again to relativism as the safest and sanest finality, as the measure of true religion and true art:

Religion, goodness, beauty, property, and crime grade into each other though religion is the highest of this gradation. The self-belief, the love-belief, the art-belief are all related to the God-belief.[13]

Such a tone of humanistic relativism finds its best test of eternity in the quality of human love. In all of Frost's poetry, however simple and reasonable, the reader always gets the impression that the poet is "one who cares." His is a modest sincerity without sentimentality. He cannot easily give up the old loves of his life, and he admits his weakness in "Reluctance" . . . "to bow and accept the end/Of a love or a season." Of his personal love, never so mentioned by name in his poetry, he speaks only by synecdochical displacement in which the strong sentiment is revealed by a single image or incident as in "The Tuft of Flowers," "Meeting and Passing," "Two Look at Two," and "In Neglect." Never blatant, these modulations of tone and texture range from the quiet loyalty of "Flower Gathering" to the intense passion of "The Subverted Flower." The metaphoric details by which love is expressed may be the first simple invitation to walk to "The Pasture"; the germination and development of "Putting in the Seed"; the fulfillment of "Love and a Question" or "Two Look at Two"; the test of "The Trial by Existence" or of "Bond and Free"; and the final triumph of "A Prayer in Spring"—"For this is love, and nothing else is love!"

Frost recognizes the extremities to which love may be strained, and he has analyzed these crises in a rather large body of his poetry. "Nothing Gold Can Stay," "The Telephone," "West-Running Brook," and "Hill Wife" are all good examples of his variations on this theme. The theoretical perfection of love is best represented in "Moon Compasses," "On the Heart's Beginning to Cloud the Mind," and "The Silken Tent"; while "To Earthward" and "Wild Grapes" recognize the basic and necessary futility of man's efforts to achieve perfect union. This "Yankee" lover who quarrels with the world assures his readers, "All my poems are love poems," and the sympathetic reader is able to catch the significance of the many different nuances of this love as it moves between physical desire and Platonic union.

It is the reader's pleasure to catch the mood of a Frost poem: to experience "the triumph to be reminded"—his own triumph as well as Frost's—when the moods of both can coincide in humor, skepticism, and love. Frost always hopes for the sympathetic reader who *can* catch his moods; he addresses him in the last significant lines of "To the Right Person:"

> . . . mere learning is the devil
> And this school isn't keeping any more
> Unless for penitents who take their seat
> Upon its doorstep as at mercy's feet
> To make up for a lack of meditation.

Frost expects a reader who *will* meditate, and he is not interested in the many who do not realize the "miles to go" that are needed for what he calls "successful correspondence" in the establishment of the mood of his poems. He wants his own personal idiom of poetic expression to achieve this correspondence between his own experience and the experience of those who read his poems. In spite of his stated

101

distrust of explication, here is the admitted paradox of this poet's craving both the intimacy of experience which gives insight for others and at the same time seeking the privacy of isolation which permits an objectivity and perspective all its own. He has said that he would like to withdraw into his own and guard his secrets in the "dark woods" down "the road not taken"; still he knows—as practicing poet—that "Men work together . . . whether they work together or apart."

In establishing a sympathetic contract of tone and attitude with the reader, Frost insists that the ultimate test is "how a writer takes himself." And yet as a poet, he refuses to assume any pseudo-romantic stance; he concludes with typical enigmatic paradox: " 'Know thyself' has never been one of my mottoes. I'm more objective than that.!"[14]

Part Three

His Poems

"You and I know enough to know . . .
. . . all the fun's in how you say a thing."
—"The Mountain."

When one writes about Frost, one feels lamentably sure of how lamentably short of his world one is going to fall; one can never write about him without wishing that one could talk about hundreds of poems and hundreds of other things, and fall short, by one's essential and not accidental limitations.[1]

With such an introduction Randall Jarrell quietly alerted "The Laodiceans" of 1952 about Robert Frost and published his own list of Frost favorites for explication. Within the last decade, similar renewed interest in Frost by serious critics has brought a dozen such varied lists into print to correct the trite taste of the frequently anthologized "Birches" and "Death of the Hired Man." It is, indeed, presumptuous to choose a dozen poems to represent the complete Frost; however, it seems more satisfactory to try to choose a dozen *complete* poems for analysis than to present him by broken bits of many. Subsequent chapters offer four from each of the three types of Frost's poetry: the lyric, the dramatic narrative, and the satire. The criticism of Frost has suggested that if a choice is to be made among the three, the poet may be represented at his best by the lyric, in which he seems to achieve the most complete artistic intensity. In the dramatic narrative, character development by dialogue has been one of his greatest successes—as it was Robert Browning's, whom he has greatly admired; however, his own choice for his public readings and recordings indicates that he too prefers the lyrics. The satires are most frequently successful when they allow their wit and wisdom the "fire and ice" of paradoxical contrast and concentrated form; the longer ones are likely to be rambling and didactic. In them, he sometimes sounds like a pontifical old man saying, "I've lived my life; now live yours as well if you can." Frost must be forgiven, surely, these occasional paternalisms when the complete poetry is assayed; for many of the satires are rapier-quick and wise for any age, and the great majority of the lyrics and the dramatic narratives are successful. The poems explicated in this section have been chosen for their varying levels of intensity and effect.

These poems illustrate some of Frost's most successful poetic practices, but it is notable that they also show up some of his faults in certain areas. Some of the poems are better known than others but are less frequently explicated. One from each of the three groups is very well known, and the other three from each are less familiar. Their range and varying success are apparent as they are contrasted and juxtaposed. While no effort was made to choose them from any single theme—but rather for artistic interest—it is apparent that they represent a far more serious Frost than the usual anthology selections.

The poems will be discussed in the following order: LYRICS—"Acquainted with the Night," "Stopping by Woods on a Snowy Evening," "Design," "Desert Places"; DRAMATIC NARRATIVES—"The Mountain," "A Servant to Servants," "The Witch of Coös," "Home Burial"; SATIRES—"Departmental," "Neither Out Far Nor In Deep," "Happiness Makes Up in Height," "Choose Something Like a Star."[2] (These poems may all be found in *The Complete Poems of Robert Frost*, Henry Holt, 1949.)

Chapter Eight

Lyrics

ACQUAINTED WITH THE NIGHT

I have been one acquainted with the night.
I have walked out in rain—and back in rain.
I have outwalked the furthest city light.

I have looked down the saddest city lane.
I have passed by the watchman on his beat
And dropped my eyes, unwilling to explain.

I have stood still and stopped the sound of feet
When far away an interrupted cry
Came over houses from another street,

But not to call me back or say good-by;
And further still at an unearthly height,
One luminary clock against the sky

Proclaimed the time was neither wrong nor right.
I have been one acquainted with the night.

With a simple, direct statement the poet introduces the mood and subject matter for his lyric, a statement so simple and direct that the flatness seems to assume at the outset a reader's undersanding and to see no additional reason to qualify itself. There is the sonorous quality of the long vowels in the accented beats to set the musical tone in his first statement: the metrical variations suggest a mood of hesitation; the metaphoric "night" sets the image for the entire poem; and the simple thematic personification of "I" implies Everyman. So in the first sentence the poem's pattern is set. The fugue-like development is formally interlocked by the use of *terza rima,* in which the use of run-on lines and conversational diction makes this formal pattern almost imperceptible orally. It is a lyric in which form is precisely apparent to the eye and unobtrusively helpful to the ear. It is one in which Frost's idea and mood of classic acceptance and romantic regret are brought together. The poem is kept within the bounds of simple, everyday statement and image; within these bounds, it strives to experience precisely the essence of man's existence in his lonely human state. As such, it becomes a universal elegy for mankind's aspirations as well as one man's personal lament.

The poem develops after the first statement's psalm-like intonation with a series of repetitions: five "I have" clauses to make specific the details of a man of sorrow, acquainted with grief. The interesting metrical variations in the lines of these "I have" clauses contribute to their meaning. The first foot in each one is a trochee followed by an iamb—which puts the emphasis on "I" and "One" with a natural caesura at mid-line. After this hesitation, this attempt at self-analysis, the line moves to a rapid, regular iambic conclusion "acquainted with the night," etc. The irregularity and slowed rhythm of the first two feet emphasize the difficulty of the seeker who tries to explain himself, and who finally resolves his explanation in the last three regular feet that continue through the entire sequence. These are simple statements—"I have been"—for the basic state-of-being verb, the most common word in any language. They are in the present-perfect tense to suggest finality of the past as well as potentiality, positive or negative, for the future.

The favorite Frost symbols are here, the simple images of complete loneliness in night rain as opposed to the semi-security of light and people. The lonely speaker indicates his spiritual anguish as he ignores his physical discomfort. "I have walked out in rain - and back in rain" accents the contrast of "out and back" with the constancy of the repeated rain each way. "I have outwalked the furthest city light"; the poet has in his solitary effort left the confines of civilization, the last vestiges of urban men and their secure lights which shine for such a little way; and out in the dark he has sought his own soul. Even upon return, the lighted city is saddest of all for him; and he is forced to deny the guardian of man's own efforts to protect and shelter himself. Self-consciously he must even drop his eyes before the watchman of the night who could not be expected to understand the yearning of this man who walks his streets looking and listening for surcease. Here is another human man like himself; and yet, "unwilling to explain," he cannot speak to him or even meet his eyes through the veil of his own solitude. Even his own motion seems a hindrance to the quest, and he stands still to test the silence for the reality of the "interrupted cry," the potential answer to the ever-listening, ever-seeking lonely heart. Onomatopoetically, the line also hushes the reader who waits in suspense as he hears the 'st' sounds in "I have stood still and stopped the sound of feet." The cry that comes to him is not close by, not recognizable, not certain . . . "over houses from another street" . . . "interrupted" . . . , and it is impossible for him to define exactly where or what it is that seems to lure him. The cry is not that of human kind calling him back for happy reunion; neither is it sad farewell. It can be given no human identification or recognition in the mind of mortal man.

Five direct, flat, repetitious statements to support the initial statement all end in periods of declarative honesty. They build to a climax of detailed negation. The first is simple enough: leaving in the loneliness of rain and so returning; the second, outwalking the furthest city light beyond the range of human association; the third, looking down the saddest city lane disassociated from general humanity near at hand; the fourth, dropping his eyes before the watchman, rejecting contact with another "normal" human representing care and caution; and finally trying to disassociate himself entirely from even his own bodily motion, his own living, in his search for essence. The variation noted in the sixth statement's projection and development emphasizes this climax of spiritual anguish. The lonely man hears the faraway, interrupted cry which he can almost catch, not from any loved human tones or terms . . . "but over houses from another street." And "further still at an unearthly height," he sees ironically the last final symbol of man's precarious efforts to measure and control the universe—"to tell time"—to mark it right or wrong according to his own presumptuous mechanical standards. "One luminary clock against the sky" shines in its little man-made brilliance, too high, too small, hanging against the vast darkness which he can never fathom if he has only his simple trust in the moment of the mechanical hands pointing the mechanical hour. This is the last rejection of all. The time *is* "neither wrong nor right"; the answer has not come through in the interrupted cry; he has not heard beyond the confines of human understanding however much he may strain and wish. The cry was there to catch, but the ears and mind were interrupted. So he must go back, unsatisfied, to looking at mere human mechanisms, at controlled, well-wound, certain understandable symbols which he knows are neither wrong nor right but are only man's compromise with relative truth. And it is not enough. In his basic humility that sends him seeking beyond the restraints of his own mind, he states again flatly the one thing which he knows for sure: "I have been one acquainted with the night." It has been and will be a forever lonely search for the sensitive human who tries to transcend his mortal environment, and it will end only with human death. Here is Frost, the master of isolation poetry, making the "sound of sense" with both content and form as the mood is evoked.

So the poem builds to a final repetition of the initial refrain with the assurance of a fugue's coda. Man may proclaim by his own devices his own attempts to understand the universe; what he proclaims seems neither wrong nor right as yet to this seeker. His night is no less dark for being familiar; and yet he will never reject the acknowledged dark until the cry and the light are seen and heard in true knowledge. The partial cannot suffice, although the search for complete understanding is a lonely "road not taken" by most. The final couplet breaks the *terza rima* with a grim finality showing the actual sonnet form which though unusual in line division, is none-the-less effective in its climax.

DESERT PLACES

Snow falling and night falling fast, oh, fast
In a field I looked into going past,
And the ground almost covered smooth in snow,
But a few weeds and stubble showing last.

The woods around it have it—it is theirs.
All animals are smothered in their lairs.
I am too absent-spirited to count;
The loneliness includes me unawares.

And lonely as it is that loneliness
Will be more lonely ere it will be less—
A blanker whiteness of benighted snow
With no expression, nothing to express.

They cannot scare me with their empty spaces
Between stars—on stars where no human race is.
I have it in me so much nearer home
To scare myself with my own desert places.

In this poem Frost presents one of his visual snowscapes: full of whiteness, of monochromatic quiet, of muted monosyllables that paint the picture. What appears to be only an equally quiet, reserved structure of simple four-line stanzas serves the same quiet purpose; yet both content and form come to surprising climax by the end of the poem. The form never deviates from the tone, mood, and subject matter except as the author allows the sound of sense to tell the tale in the voice of the lonely speaker who talks to himself through the thick, heavy snow. The difficult rhyme scheme that repeats three times in each stanza's four lines assists by its repetition the hypnotic, smothering quality of the poem. The spirit of the man, heavy and thick with fear, is not mentioned until the sixth line, although it is apparent from the first, another evidence of Frost's technique of assuming his reader's empathic response as a sensitive human to the gloom painted in preceding lines. It is an almost completely horizontal scene—the images are of vast stretches of snow and night and level fields and low stubble. All these things on a clear day may be seen beyond, and some comfort may be gained from the wide horizon or the high stars. But on this night, only the immediate present of the enclosed spirit shut in by snow like the smothered animal is perceived; and that spirit, "too absent-spirited to count," has lost track of its relation to the rest of the animal or human world. The landscape has numbed and reduced its sensibility.

With the fricative "f" sound in the first two lines the poet represents the spirit fighting humanly against the inevitability of the motion of the snow; and with the "l's" of the second and third lines it seems lulled to acceptance. As the poem opens, this spirit notes the mechanical slanting fall of the snow across the flattened world, and the "fast, oh fast" propels the poem urgently in the man's voice pattern to match the inexorable fall of dark. The ground itself has lost contour, and heights and depths seem all one level thought as the sheer hypnosis of cold and whiteness sets in. The second stanza abandons the rest of the world to the snow, Frost's favorite image for death. "The woods around it have it—it is theirs." But what is the "it?" The very conversational quality of the poem has taken the reader unaware, and he is asked suddenly to understand this "it" with no antecedent, to enter the writer's mind and mood and recognize "it" as the loneliness which appears in its phonetic desolation and includes "me" in the last line of the second stanza. Suddenly the range of the poem is diminished internally; the wide spatial solitude is now pinpointed within the lonely-spirited sayer. He looks within as well as without and finds no break, no interruption in either direction for his own isolation.

In the third stanza, the mathematically perfect form which has presented the two lonelinesses now balances them for four lines; it contrasts "that" loneliness without with "this" within. The snow will continue to fall all through the night to increase that loneliness "ere it will be less"; but it can be counted on to cease eventually. The "benighted" snow—literally "caught or surrounded by night"—serves the purpose of contrast. It is also figuratively the pointless snow, without direction, without mental or spiritual impulse; unenlightened as to its own state, it will start to fall and stop many times in the future without direction or self-motivation, "with no expression, nothing to express." Suddenly in the last stanza, the *non*-benighted man, with a great deal to express seems to realize his own potentialities and to experience stark self-recognition. He is capable of facing his own isolation and desperation, his own unknown depths. "They" are as anony-

109

mous as "it" before—and in true simple diction of man speaking, the "they" remains a grammatical and poetic mystery. "They cannot scare me with their empty spaces/ Between stars—on stars where no human race is." "They" may be scientists, theologians, or even fellow-poets; this man stands up to them. The lines balance in perfect parallels of rhythm and rhyme when read aloud with the proper pause for reflection as the punctuated thought indicates. In defiance of all the "theys" of science or religion, with simple humble fact opposed to pontifical erudite authority, this "lone-spirited" man looks into his own depths and finds desert places to match "so much nearer home"; in a curious about-face, he rather proudly takes courage from his own known abysses which can match any universal depths. The very colloquial use of the word "scare" acknowledges the potential fear, child-like and common to all men who can never know with reason and who can only trust with faith. "To scare myself" is the fate of every man who is at all honest with himself. And this man is so honest that he uses the vernacular to express this realization. Rhythmically, the last line is a *tour de force of accents* adroitly placed to fall on "myself" and "own." How can his spirit revel in its own loneliness, "with no expression, nothing to express"? There has come to him the peace of acceptance, the mystical acquaintance with his own desert places so that their very acknowledgment and resignation regenerate a kind of strength that is more than sheer fatalism.

STOPPING BY WOODS
ON A SNOWY EVENING

Whose woods these are I think I know.
His house is in the village though;
He will not see me stopping here
To watch his woods fill up with snow.

My little horse must think it queer
To stop without a farmhouse near
Between the woods and frozen lake
The darkest evening of the year.

He gives his harness bells a shake
To ask if there is some mistake.
The only other sound's the sweep
Of easy wind and downy flake.

The woods are lovely, dark and deep,
But I have promises to keep,
And miles to go before I sleep,
And miles to go before I sleep.

This is probably the best known and the most misunderstood of Frost's poems. Its last lines have attracted critics for years and puzzled Frost's popular audience. Frost says he wrote the poem in a state of fatigue and euphoria after working all night on a longer poem and that this one seemed almost spontaneous in its swift creation. When asked about the repeated last line at the end, Frost is supposed to have said he "only wanted to go home" and that he had been "stuck for a last line." This is the sort of answer he might be expected to give to people who would obviously only be able to understand it in those terms.

The poem, the poet's own reading of it, and his remarks about it all indicate that the theme itself concerns the location of this very "home" for poet and reader. What is it to which he has been returning dutifully all these years in spite of the lovely, dark and deep woods? Why are the promises of the third stanza that were made before the temptation still stronger than it is? Why are they strong enough to evoke first of all the casual, conversational, reasonable first statement in its everyday "sound of sense"? "But I have promises to keep/ And miles to go before I sleep." Then abruptly Frost suggests a sudden change of voice and mood value as he repeats the last line in his own reading of the poem; so that the promises of the last line are *not* the same mundane duties to others as are those of the practical third line. By now, with metaphysical extension in the fourth line, they become the promises of the spirit to itself; and they lament the miles to go to keep them, for the creative, curious mind will not let go until the quest has been fulfilled. Reason or faith alone is not enough to justify returning home satisfied or staying away unworried; some compromise or combination must be sought.

The poem begins as the poet makes his familiar way home with a little horse who knows every turn. It is not necessary to be guided "home"; and the little horse knows, as the traveller meditates at a stop before the lonely woods, that this is only a temporary rest. The tone at the beginning is established by conversational diction which carries the sort of stream-of-consciousness commentary in which any traveller indulges as he rides alone past familiar sights; and yet he looks at these woods with more than usual affection, for this traveller knows these woods much better than their city owner—not as a financial but as a spiritual investment. Actually, he *is* their owner in spirit, recalling with familiarity their many past temptations and delights. The favorite sight is—for poet-traveller—much more of a "coming home" than for the villager-owner, who perhaps has never stopped to watch his woods fill up with snow. The poet delights in his solitary indulgence as he stops to watch; and it pleases him in a sceret sort of way that the real owner will never know his stolen pleasure. The image of the woods "filling up" with snow is one of silent motion that suggests the unrealized speed and force of this natural element as it rises in depth on tree-levels and fields. Dark is falling as fast as is the snow; the woods are fast filling with the mystery of both. The poet, Man, capable of dreaming beyond the immediate reality, is attracted and almost hypnotized by the blank whiteness, and for the moment the prosaic necessity of getting on with the day's duties leaves him. He is suspended in this world of white silence, lured toward the dark deep woods where there are no practical limits of cause and effect to be considered, no responsibility for choices even for himself.

The first stanza ends with the poet's letting himself stop to look at the sight which has long been loved; and the second stanza breaks abruptly into the meditation. Frost, in many of his poems, poses the physical reactions of the animal world against those of man to point up the contrasting stark reality of life—the reasonableness of it—lived at the plane of sheer necessity of "my little horse." The second and third stanzas contain two-line alternations of counterpoint between the natural animal reactions of the horse to weather and landscape and the spiritual interpretations of the lonely man to the symbols of death and mystery around him. Each stanza breaks between second and third lines in this dialogue of juxtaposed meditations. The speaker's affectionate attitude toward his horse is important in characterizing himself and in hardening the poem's drift toward romanticism. The man speaks fondly of the animal who is so nearly human that he can almost read his master's thoughts; indeed the master invests him with a consciousness all his own and supposes his limited thoughts—"must think it queer," etc. . . He gives his horse all the necessary rational thought processes for what would be considered a "normal" human reaction. "Why get home?" "For security, warmth, comfort, food." "Why stay here watching the silent woods full of cold snow by a frozen lake in the dark?" At the actual mundane level "the darkest evening of the year" is around Christmas; at the spiritual level, it is the darkest in the poet's life as he contemplates death-in-life. The horse knows enough to shake the harness bells, to rouse the dreamer, to question the dream. Nature resents such dreaming deviation from her pattern; realists will find the snow colder than it is white and beautiful, the woods darker and deeper than they are lovely. And realists *and* dreamers will both have to pay the same natural penalty if they stay too long. If there were other humans to help, another farmhouse even near, such a risk might be well taken, such a dare afforded; but not now, not here. On one side, dark woods; on the other, frozen lake; and the darkest evening of the year well along. Any reader who has passed middle age will recognize the images and the cautious tendency toward withdrawal. Impending tragedy suggests itself and is almost attractive in its temptation. Sensible creatures seek shelter and acknowledge their debt to the warnings of nature however inimically kind. Obeisance is made, and reason stays in its proper place. The little horse stands here against this landscape with the little man—but with the great difference of the dream between them.

The cheerful sound of the harness bells shaking and the mournful sound of the sweep of "easy wind" are contrasted, and the structure begins to be more and more apparent for its series of parallels: first the city owner of the woods who stays in town or the traveller who stops happily by the woods; the little horse with his animal instinct, or the man with his daring impracticalities; the well-known ringing of the harness bells' warning, or the unknown sweep and moan of nature luring him beyond the immediate horizon of the woods' edge. Beyond is constant quiet—the dark deep loveliness that offers nothing sure and seems to prophesy only danger. Although the poet-traveller ruefully admits, "The woods are lovely, dark and deep," he shakes himself back to reality with the well-rehearsed line that he has so often said to himself when temptation threatened. He repeats this line, familiar in content to men everywhere as he manages somehow to talk himself into the less attractive, the safer, saner rationalization for this familiar weak moment. Quietly desperate but practical, he recalls, "But I have promises to keep." One imagines this line read in a kind of sing-song intonation that almost borders on unconscious irony because it is so thoughtless, so often repeated without thinking: "And miles to go before I sleep." And man can at least await that sleep—"whatever sleep it be." So the artist gives up the dream, the philosopher gives up the answer . . . but not willingly or easily.

Suddenly having said the familiar line out of habit, having assured himself in his everyday voice, with the well-worn, age-old axiom of practicality and security, he realizes how it not only fits his immediate problem as he objectifies his duties to others, but how well it also fits his own inner spiritual problems. He muses over the implications of the last line's repetition. There are other promises made that are not all a matter of taking home groceries and putting away horses; there are promises to himself and to his own soul, and it will not do to give up to the dark woods and "come in" until, bearing it out to the edge of doom, he has traversed the miles to go and kept these promises too. Then his sleep will be the final one, the one that is neither premeditated nor entered into by volition against nature; though the dark lovely depths do seem to promise more at the moment than the eventual long journey home.

The poem is written in a difficult variant of *terza rima;* it is held together between stanzaic patterns by an interlocking rhyme scheme in which the new rhyme of each stanza provides the main rhyme for the next until the final climactic repetition at the end. The poem's scansion and diction are as calm, as apparently tranquil as its very images and pattern of thought. Its rhythmic calm assures this very paradoxical comfort of the last mile as something to be endured ʰy all men and understood before sleep is known.

It suggests to the artist or the critic another interpretation besides the philosophic one—one of an *ars poetica* itself; and perhaps as such it fulfills Frost's own dictum that an entire poem always be a symbol. . . "the figure a poem makes" is here one of conventionality—the "sound of sense" poetically. The lovely, dark, deep woods might conceivably be the limitless, free range of associational interpretations toward which all artists and critics naturally lean. The miles and promises in such a symbolism would then be the strictures of form and content that recall the esoteric poet's flights back to the necessary communication of understandable ideas and images to his readers. But perhaps just such an interpretation is guilty of yielding to the same temptation against which its very images warn!

DESIGN

I found a dimpled spider, fat and white,
On a white heal-all, holding up a moth
Like a white piece of rigid satin cloth—
Assorted characters of death and blight
Mixed ready to begin the morning right,
Like the ingredients of a witches' broth—
A snow-drop spider, a flower like a froth,
And dead wings carried like a paper kite.

What had that flower to do with being white,
The wayside blue and innocent heal-all?
What brought the kindred spider to that height,
Then steered the white moth thither in the night?
What but design of darkness to appall?—
If design govern in a thing so small.

In this poem Frost uses the rigidity of a formal sonnet to present the rigidity of a formal philosophic problem. It is a poem whose pattern has the scientific precision and method of a syllogism or of a geometric theorem, and it is as carefully concluded. In the octet, the three elements are introduced individually, assembled in synthesis to show their incongruous relation and repeated in the last two lines for emphasis. Thus far the scientist-poet allows himself only the emotional shock of the juxtaposition of these elements presented under his eye's microscope; and he accepts them, as nature has posed them, as specimens at random. It is when he begins to solve the problem, to analyze the elements, that the tension breaks (as the sonnet itself breaks) in the careful scientist's mind, and he becomes at this moment the philosopher-poet who demands reason for the weird combinations of existence. In the search for some design to interpret, the poet is brought face to face with a shocking realization concerning scientific evolution and philosophic fatalism. He comes to his conclusion by a series of negations, a series of outraged rhetorical questions that his mind asks and for which there seems to be only one obvious answer. Then suddenly the inverted pyramid of questions comes tumbling down in the last cold, calculated thrust of the subjunctive clause that qualifies the entire poem and problem.

The poet recounts an accident—or rather a coincidence of nature upon which he stumbles most casually and by which he is shaken emotionally. His reasoning mind cannot account for it by statistics, laws of supply and demand, or evolutionary theories; his faith can hardly believe that such a design can be so intended, even malevolently. However, worse than such an intended design might be is the suspicious horror of the last line's *un*designed fatality. It exists, and it must be understood by a simple acceptance of its essence; as such it represents one of the best examples of Frost's existential poetry. Perhaps there is an even more casual explanation than undesigned fatality . . . no explanation at all. And here the poet probes the limits of man's thinking to mock him with the very futility of reason *or* faith. These are indeed the "desert places" of man's heart and mind.

The poem is all the more effective for its apparent artlessness, the simplicity of its incident, and its unobtrusive characters. These are not thinking humans waging premeditated wars. These are the natural enemies of the animal world who might be expected to attack each other by instinct; the tiny, incidental and thereby more horrifying actors in this drama of life and death. The very presumption of the incident's possibility—once in a million chances—is what makes the observing, thinking man so helpless before it. He ponders the improbability of nature's mixing such a brew on such a morning. How *can* it be "designed"? And yet how much more horrible if it is so! The "dimpled spider"—"fat and white" with its paradoxical adjectives of innocent purity—*happens* to be on the white flower—the flower ironically called the "heal-all' that is only white this one time by some genetic accident of coloration. This flower *should* be blue in a normally designed natural world, the safe blue of the many others like it that cover the roadside indiscriminately. But this *one* is white, and its whiteness matches that of the grim actors in this drama of death on its stage. They all exhibit the non-color quality which for Frost is so commonly linked symbolically with snow, isolation, and death. This is whiteness with or without reason; and herein lies the mystery. It may be the deception of white, the never-never land of the prism or the shroud; it may be the purity of white, the virgin innocence; it may be the albino deviation of a worshipped idol different from the norm— a Moby Dick arachnid. Whatever "white" may mean in the history of man's thought, here it finally means the *raison d'être* for death itself. The white, fat spider, obscene but somehow attractive, poised precariously and delicately on the white flower, carries the stiff, dead-white wings of the fragile moth still bent as a kite, ready for immediate flight back to life.

The sheer understatement of the accident gives it its power and terror. The almost-but-not-quite possibility of this luminous trio, brought together out of the huge gloom of a dark universe and spotlighted before the wary eye of the poet, magnifies the coincidence from microscopic to macroscopic terror in his mind. Here is Frost's metaphysical extension rapidly achieved. If this incident can possibly have been planned and designed, then it is impossibly terrifying. But even such a possibility can be guarded against in the human world with skill and facility. But the wary poet asks himself four rhetorical questions with mounting emotion to try to convince himself. Finally he faces the ultimate possibility. If it is *un*-planned, then life is utterly desolate in connotation; and thinking man must reject this idea if he will live with sanity and die wth faith. The poet does not assume the conclusion in the finality of a declarative sentence; he only alludes to the possibility in the potential of a subjunctive clause. He takes no responsibility beyond that of a scientist for presenting the possibilities to a philosopher. But he mixes a poetic witches' broth all his own out of the symbolic scene.

The white flower that provides the draped bier sets the stage. Assorted characters of death and blight are the images ironically mixed. Impossibly brought together out of their usual elements, they are here ready to begin this "morning right" like any other morning, unaware of their own particular *danse macabre*. The man watching is forced to wonder when and where his own particular dance may be so arranged —so "designed"—in the universal scheme of which he is sure he is a part; an arrangement for the design of death seems to give him certain satisfaction. The grotesque scene on this cheerful "right" morning creates a mounting irony. The simile "like the ingredients of a witches' broth" increases the horror, and the last three innocent victims of the octet's last line are conclusive and deadly in their ironic parallelism under the poet's microscope. It is as though they marched across the stage of his instrument according to their listing in his last sentence. From here on, anything can happen; the scientist waits with disinterested eye to record their pattern on his chart. These are teasing images full of paradox; they should be used by any reasonable, traditional poet to describe beauty, happiness, or design to be beheld for its own joyful sake: "a snowdrop spider"—a kind of a caricature of his malevolent black brother; a "flower like a froth"—froth of delicate beauty and decay; the rigid satin holding up the "dead wings carried like a paper kite"—fragility, stiffness, wind-borne delicacy, transience of all life which is suddenly here *rigor mortis*. Here there *might* have been beauty and design to behold for its own joyful sake. But in the mind of the beholder who looks and thinks twice there can be only death, perhaps even *un*-designed death. This poem does in fourteen lines a far more effective job than does "The Lesson for Today" in hundreds on this same theme of *memento mori*.

The sestet forces the enraged, insulted observer to seek a contact with a Creator, any creator or designer of a universe in which such a thing can happen. He demands with direct questions an explanation for the white silence of the scene. Why were the three kindred in their abnormality to begin with, and what malevolent force brought them together for their end? "Steered" and "brought" imply direction and a premeditated pattern; "thither to that height" implies foresight and judgment. Such questions, always posed in the fury of any incident or accident by which man's small intelligence has been insulted, are answered in the cold, calm couplet at the end of the sonnet which here so perfectly—as perfectly and formally as death itself—serves its artistic function. "What but design of darkness to appall?" the poet asks his reader. If this *is* then a purposeful horror, an intended design of destiny, the reader might try to summon a little stoic calm with which to defy fright. If it *is* "design of darkness," he might still kindle an inner light with some temporary charity and good works on this earth. But just as he is trying to dredge up some satisfactory answer in his own mind, to salvage something with which to live to face a similar horror himself . . . the *coup de grace* is struck in the last line's casual, quiet suspicion: "*If* design govern in a thing so small." The man is left gaping in his *own* miniature situation in the universe. It has been his particular fame and fate to suppose and assume design, to acknowledge pattern, to proclaim and imitate it always in one way or another in his science and his art. "In the beginning Someone created the heavens and the earth," he has said with confidence; he has continued to claim design right down to the last fissionable molecule of that earth. And now the poet suggests that this thinking man realize the moment of his *own* desperation when he too faces the possible horror of being left out of his own universe with his mind trailing behind

117

him. And as the great "perhaps" of *any* design rises to haunt him, it is left for him to be even more casually courageous, to bear the simplicity of the "if" for a "thing so small" as he now knows himself to be. He is left with whatever tragic heroism his own existential glory may be able to summon.

Chapter Nine

Dramatic Narratives

THE MOUNTAIN

The mountain held the town as in a shadow.
I saw so much before I slept there once;
I noticed that I missed stars in the west,
Where its black body cut into the sky.
Near me it seemed; I felt it like a wall
Behind which I was sheltered from a wind.
And yet between the town and it I found,
When I walked forth at dawn to see new things,
Were fields, a river, and beyond, more fields.
The river at the time was fallen away,
And made a widespread brawl on cobblestones;
But the signs showed what it had done in spring:
Good grassland gullied out, and in the grass
Ridges of sand, and driftwood stripped of bark.
I crossed the river and swung round the mountain.
And there I met a man who moved so slow
With white-faced oxen in a heavy cart,
It seemed no harm to stop him altogether.

'What town is this?' I asked.

       'This? Lunenburg.'

 Then I was wrong: the town of my sojourn,
Beyond the·bridge, was not that of the mountain,
But only felt at night its shadowy presence.
'Where is your village? Very far from here?'

'There is no village—only scattered farms.
We were but sixty voters last election.
We can't in nature grow to many more:
That thing takes all the room!' He moved his goad.
The mountain stood there to be pointed at.
Pasture ran up the side a little way,
And then there was a wall of trees with trunks;

After that only tops of trees, and cliffs
Imperfectly concealed among the leaves.
A dry ravine emerged from under boughs
Into the pasture.

      'That looks like a path.
Is that the way to reach the top from here?—
Not for this morning, but some other time:
I must be getting back to breakfast now.'

'I don't advise your trying from this side.
There is no proper path, but those that have
Been up, I understand, have climbed from Ladd's.
That's five miles back. You can't mistake the place:
They logged it there last winter some way up.
I'd take you, but I'm bound the other way.'

'You've never climbed it?'

       'I've been on the sides,
Deer-hunting and trout-fishing. There's a brook
That starts up on it somewhere—I've heard say
Right on the top, tip-top—a curious thing.
But what would interest you about the brook,
It's always cold in summer, warm in winter.
One of the great sights going is to see
It steam in winter like an ox's breath.
Until the bushes all along its banks
Are inch-deep with the frosty spines and bristles—
You know the kind. Then let the sun shine on it!'

'There ought to be a view around the world
From such a mountain—if it isn't wooded
Clear to the top.' I saw through leafy screens
Great granite terraces in sun and shadow,
Shelves one could rest a knee on getting up—
With depths behind him sheer a hundred feet.
Or turn and sit on and look out and down,
With little ferns in crevices at his elbow.

'As to that I can't say. But there's the spring,
Right on the summit, almost like a fountain.
That ought to be worth seeing.'

       'If it's there.
You never saw it?'

       'I guess there's no doubt
About it's being there. I never saw it.
It may not be right on the very top:
It wouldn't have to be a long way down
To have some head of water from above,

And a *good distance* down might not be noticed
By anyone who'd come a long way up.
One time I asked a fellow climbing it
To look and tell me later how it was.'

'What did he say?'

'He said there was a lake
Somewhere in Ireland on a mountain top.'

'But a lake's different. What about the spring?'

'He never got up high enough to see.
That's why I don't advise your trying this side.
He tried this side. I've always meant to go
And look myself, but you know how it is:
It doesn't seem so much to climb a mountain
You've worked around the foot of all your life.
What would I do? Go in my overalls,
With a big stick, the same as when the cows
Haven't come down to the bars at milking time?
Or with a shotgun for a stray black bear?
'Twouldn't seem real to climb for climbing it.'

'I shouldn't climb it if I didn't want to—
Not for the sake of climbing. What's its name?'

'We call it Hor: I don't know if that's right.'

'Can one walk around it? Would it be too far?'

'You can drive round and keep in Lunenburg,
But it's as much as ever you can do,
The boundary lines keep in so close to it.
Hor is the township, and the township's Hor—
And a few houses sprinkled round the foot,
Like boulders broken off the upper cliff,
Rolled out a little farther than the rest.'

'Warm in December, cold in June, you say?'

'I don't suppose the water's changed at all.
You and I know enough to know it's warm
Compared with cold, and cold compared with warm
But all the fun's in how you say a thing.'

'You've lived here all your life?'

'Ever since Hor
Was no bigger than a—' What, I did not hear.
He drew the oxen toward him with light touches
Of his slim goad on nose and offside flank,
Gave them their marching orders and was moving.

121

Frost's particular effort in his dramatic narratives is to sound "like men talking" and to think like men thinking. In this one he achieves the calm, meditative, every-day quality of strangers meeting casually without any particular emotional reaction, exchanging a few words on the roadside, and parting without further ado. Actually, not much happens here in the way of action, and the drama lies in the thought conflicts hinted at but barely expressed. From this dialogue come the distinct strains of two highly individualized characters and their philosophies of life. It is a "flat" poem in Frost's "loose iamb" of conversational pentameter. The rhythms are carefully yet unobtrusively preserved throughout the speech by line-breaks so that no tags are necessary for understanding and no interruptions intrude metrically except the necessary ones of the human voice speaking or reading the lines with pauses, accents, and italics to preserve the tone. This "tone" makes it one of Frost's most subtle dialogues as it contrasts two ways of life in two men's minds.

The title suggests that the mountain is the subject of the poem, not the men or the meeting; and it becomes clear in the first line that it will serve as "constant symbol." The poem opens with a sentence that immediately sets the pattern for the omnipresent mountain's influence on both the men, who are held momentarily in its shadow, and the townsmen, who live in it constantly. The second line introduces the strange visitor and characterizes him quickly as a meditative dreamer and artist without actually saying so. He is simply presented as the kind of man who *would* notice these things, who would miss stars in the west and feel the dark shadow of the wall cut the wind from the outside world's contact. Here Frost makes use of the lessons learned so well from Shakespeare's dramas: to let the character show through the dialogue and action without long exposition, and to sketch him quickly with a few selective details. The tone of the details is always that of simple observation, of a reticent poet who goes only half way to tell them for their face value, if that is all they are to bring to the casual reader. For the inquiring mind, there are stored here metaphoric implications that continue to unfold as the poem progresses. The stranger walks forth at dawn "to see new things," and the new things seen are not just a dried-up river, but rather a "brawl on cobblestones." All the observations in the lines reflect this man's astute sense of the geography he interprets. Intricate, precise descriptions of landscape are drawn for onomatopoetic effect; the alliterative "good grassland gullied out" carries the reader along with the man's eye as together the two cross the river and swing round the mountain. By the time the stranger encounters the old native, the poet has the reader where he wants him—on the stranger's side in the conversation that follows. The old man appears, and the only description is that of his slowness; the poet, respecting the privacy and reticence of the man, asks only for direct information. And he gets only

122

direct, laconic answers. Such conversations do not spring easily into flower in this locale. It takes a quiet parrying, a slow, Yankee reserve, a "feel" for the proper questions; and eventually they bring more than just answers; they elicit additional philosophic commentary. The old man has always accepted the slow, limited state of nature here as dominated by the mountain; he has grown up with it, almost before it. Yet it is the ever-present mystery of his life: not one that he ever expects to solve or even to investigate, though he shows himself to be intelligent and curious about it and to have an almost mystic sense of power. When he says, "That thing takes all the room," it is not in resentment but rather somehow in admiration, in a kind of perverse local pride at being able to exist so long in its awesome shadow and to respect it without questioning it all these years.

When necessary, Frost injects sufficient physical description between parts of the dialogue to provide the reader with the feeling of slow conversation after much thinking before cautious talking. After some minor detail about geography, some advice about security, some local wisdom as to trails and woodlore, the careful questioner says in mild amazement, "You've never climbed it?" By this time the native's reserves are down, his confidence won, and the wonderful story about the brook spills out. The man who has all these years lived at the foot of the mountain has cherished the image of the magical brook at its very top much as a worshipper cherishes a myth about his idol. The brook evokes more than the ordinary natural or scientific fascination in him; and yet he is afraid to go and see it, to approach it in any practical way. He prefers to know it only from the mystic details of the frosty branches, the steam in winter, and the chill in summer all the better for never having seen it except as magnified in his faithful mind's eye. When he exclaims, "Then let the light shine on it!" it is with as much pride as though a Creator had just cried confidently, "Let there be light!"

Further details of conversation point the antithesis of character. The watchful stranger has already examined the base, sides, and rock plateaus at the top of the mountain; and he suggests mildly that the local man might have done likewise. But this native's interests have never really been in the mundane fishing and hunting that he has done on the lower slopes; and as to the view around the world from the top . . . he's hardly interested in *that* either. "As to that, I can't say, but there's a spring. . ." and he is again strangely and vaguely happy in his absorption with this wonderful magical phenomenon of nature that he knows is there but upon which he can never bring himself to look. His faith is sufficient in the tales brought down to make him a constant believer and a dreamer. He knows that a good distance down might not be noted by one having come a long way up. His proverbial wisdom seems somehow philosophical in a vicarious sort of way. He is full of practical wood-lore; he knows

123

mountains and their climbing; yet he has asked others to do his looking for him.

The reader and the stranger ask simultaneously the obvious question that leads directly to the heart of the poem's meaning. Why has he not gone himself?" "I've always meant to go. . ." and then the saddest revelation of all is made by this man; this potential rustic artist, dreamer, creator who cannot face his own inspiration himself, knowing his futility, feeling his lack of "difference" which he admires in the stranger. "You know how it is. . . It doesn't seem so much to climb a mountain/ You've worked around the foot of all your life." One is always embarrassed to make something ceremonial out of the everyday; only poets can make ritual out of routine without feeling foolish. It is not for the common man to be starry-eyed on his own hearthstone or to go with open-eyed wonder and naïveté about his own backyard. It's all right for the stranger; he can afford the wonderment of a tourist. But the local primitive must worship at home from afar; and this is the sad paradox. He is so doomed to live and wonder and worship only in his mind's eye out of sheer respect for fact and common sense. "What would I do? Go in my overalls?" This would be a ridiculous desecration. Yet anything more would be affectation. There would have to be some sort of masquerading justification: for a purpose, for a fact—with a gun or a stick to bolster his embarrassment over such an expedition. And yet this man is too honest with himself to create such a masquerade; when he goes—if he ever does —it must be in the spirit of pure delight and worship, that of a poet who goes simply to revel in the magic itself: not with any mundane instruments of irreverent everyday labor that would be the only plausible excuses for making the climbing seem "real." And having lived in its shadow always, he cannot now climb up to see its magic summit. (The metaphysical lengths to which this image may be carried are almost limitless: the contrast of any neophyte rich in the glory of his recent conversion or discovery as opposed to the shy diffidence of the voice-of-experience who yearns to recapture that first fine careless rapture.)

The visitor tactfully agrees that climbing merely for the sake of climbing would be unworthy; and he knows that unless the dream can be fulfilled without embarrassment the mission would indeed be of no avail. The conversation is resumed at a more comfortable plane with certainties such as names and old boundary lines. Even here the old man can hardly speak without a poetic image or two creeping into his native conversation: his description of the houses observes them "like boulders broken off the upper cliff." This man has thought in pictures all his life and has had to justify the reality of the images far beyond the limits of the here-and-now. He is a poet-primitive man who cannot identify himself in his locale because of the social structure that inhibits him. He acknowledges the stranger's oneness with himself. They are two think-

124

ing men together, two artists and philosophers. "You and I" know enough to recognize here the theory of relativity, the problem of all human aspiration set up against the absolutes of explainable fact; and the fact that the brook's temperature is a known, static thing does not in any way diminish the fancy of its magical warmth in December and chill in June. . . "But all the fun's in how you say a thing." "You and I know enough to know" that the imaginative "saying" is, after all, more fun than the actual "seeing" for these two men who feel the rapport of kindred spirits: one who has lived here all his life and one who has just come. By this time, reader identity has been established with the old native and transferred from the stranger who moves on. The last conversational bits follow in the Frost tradition of using the line breaks, mid-line caesuras, and carry-over lines to establish the "sound of sense"—that of men in casual conversation together.

The tone of the poem's end is that of quick, realistic conclusion—as typical of Frost as was the quick introduction. It shows a swift return to fact, to everyday reality lest the reader's imagination become *too* metaphorically far-fetched. The old man, embarrassed by having gone thus far with the stranger, abruptly concludes his conversation and returns to driving his oxen, who represent the plodding of his everyday existence. He is off before the stranger can catch even the last word— lost in the simile of the old man's mind forever. The fun's in having outthought, out-lived, and out-said Hor all these years anyhow! And he expects nothing better than to be buried at the foot of this mountain when he dies. He has for a little while escaped from this shadow that fascinates him though he cannot see its summit. Here is Frost's Man who successfully responds in Socratic dialogue when skillfully provoked by the right questions at the right time and who reveals the philosophy of the dreamer-humanist presented so often as the protagonist in Frost's dramatic narratives. Here is natural, normal, happy-sad man—"original" in his own "ordinary" way.

A SERVANT TO SERVANTS

I didn't make you know how glad I was
To have you come and camp here on our land.
I promised myself to get down some day
And see the way you lived, but I don't know!
With a houseful of hungry men to feed
I guess you'd find. . . It seems to me
I can't express my feelings any more
Than I can raise my voice or want to lift
My hand (oh, I can lift it when I have to).

Did ever you feel so? I hope you never.
It's got so I don't even know for sure
Whether I *am* glad, sorry, or anything.
There's nothing but a voice-like left inside
That seems to tell me how I ought to feel,
And would feel if I wasn't all gone wrong.
You take the lake. I look and look at it.
I see it's a fair, pretty sheet of water.
I stand and make myself repeat out loud
The advantages it has, so long and narrow,
Like a deep piece of some old running river
Cut short off at both ends. It lies five miles
Straight away through the mountain notch
From the sink window where I wash the plates,
And all our storms come up toward the house,
Drawing the slow waves whiter and whiter and whiter.
It took my mind off doughnuts and soda biscuit
To step outdoors and take the water dazzle
A sunny morning, or take the rising wind
About my face and body and through my wrapper,
When a storm threatened from the Dragon's Den,
And a cold chill shivered across the lake.
I see it's a fair, pretty sheet of water,
Our Willoughby! How did you hear of it?
I expect, though, everyone's heard of it.
In a book about ferns? Listen to that!
You let things more like feathers regulate
Your going and coming. And you like it here?
I can see how you might. But I don't know!
It would be different if more people came,
For then there would be business. As it is,
The cottages Len built, sometimes we rent them,
Sometimes we don't. We've a good piece of shore
That ought to be worth something, and may yet.
But I don't count on it as much as Len.
He looks on the bright side of everything,
Including me. He thinks I'll be all right
With doctoring. But it's not medicine—
Lowe is the only doctor's dared to say so—
It's rest I want—there, I have said it out—
From cooking meals for hungry hired men
And washing dishes after them—from doing
Things over and over that just won't stay done.
By good rights I ought not to have so much
Put on me, but there seems no other way.
Len says one steady pull more ought to do it.
He says the best way out is always through.
And I agree to that, or in so far

As that I can see no way out but through—
Leastways for me—and then they'll be convinced.
It's not that Len don't want the best for me.
It was his plan our moving over in
Beside the lake from where that day I showed you
We used to live—ten miles from anywhere.
We didn't change without some sacrifice,
But Len went at it to make up the loss.
His work's a man's, of course, from sun to sun,
But he works when he works as hard as I do—
Though there's small profit in comparisons.
(Women and men will make them all the same.)
But work ain't all. Len undertakes too much.
He's into everything in town. This year
It's highways, and he's got too many men
Around him to look after that make waste.
They take advantage of him shamefully,
And proud, too, of themselves for doing so.
We have four here to board, great good-for-nothings,
Sprawling about the kitchen with their talk
While I fry their bacon. Much they care!
No more put out in what they do or say
Than if I wasn't in the room at all.
Coming and going all the time, they are:
I don't learn what their names are, let alone
Their characters, or whether they are safe
To have inside the house with doors unlocked.
I'm not afraid of them, though, if they're not
Afraid of me. There's two can play at that.
I have my fancies: it runs in the family.
My father's brother wasn't right. They kept him
Locked up for years back there at the old farm.
I've been away once—yes, I've been away.
The State Asylum. I was prejudiced;
I wouldn't have sent anyone of mine there;
You know the old idea—the only asylum
Was the poorhouse, and those who could afford,
Rather than send their folks to such a place,
Kept them at home; and it does seem more human.
But it's not so: The place is the asylum.
There they have every means proper to do with,
And you aren't darkening other people's lives—
Worse than no good to them, and they no good
To you in your condition; you can't know
Affection or the want of it in that state.
I've heard too much of the old-fashioned way.
My father's brother, he went mad quite young.
Some thought he had been bitten by a dog,

127

Because his violence took on the form
Of carrying his pillow in his teeth;
But it's more likely he was crossed in love,
Or so the story goes. It was some girl.
Anyway all he talked about was love.
They soon saw he would do someone a mischief
If he wa'n't kept strict watch of, and it ended
In father's building him a sort of cage
Or room within a room of hickory poles,
Like stanchions in the barn, from floor to ceiling,—
A narrow passage all the way around.
Anything they put in for furniture
He'd tear to pieces, even a bed to lie on.
So they made the place comfortable with straw;
Like a beast's stall, to ease their consciences.
Of course they had to feed him without dishes.
They tried to keep him clothed, but he paraded
With his clothes on his arm—all of his clothes.
Cruel—it sounds. I s'pose they did the best
They knew. And just when he was at the height,
Father and mother were married, and mother came
A bride, to help take care of such a creature,
And accommodate her young life to his.
That was what marrying father meant to her.
She had to lie and hear love things made dreadful
By his shouts in the night. He'd shout and shout
Until the strength was shouted out of him,
And his voice died down slowly from exhaustion.
He'd pull his bars apart like bow and bowstring,
And let them go and make them twang until
His hands had worn them smooth as any oxbow.
And then he'd crow as if he thought that child's play
The only fun he had. I've heard them say, though,
They found a way to put a stop to it.
He was before my time—I never saw him;
But the pen stayed exactly as it was
There in the upper chamber in the ell,
A sort of catch-all full of attic clutter.
I often think of the smooth hickory bars.
It got so I would say—you know, half fooling—
'It's time I took my turn upstairs in jail'—
Just as you will till it becomes a habit.
No wonder I was glad to get away.
Mind you, I waited till Len said the word.
I didn't want the blame if things went wrong.
I was glad though, no end, when we moved out,
And I looked to be happy, and I was,
As I said, for a while—but I don't know!

Somehow the change wore out like a prescription.
And there's more to it than just window-views
And living by a lake. I'm past such help—
Unless Len took the notion, which he won't,
And I won't ask him—it's not sure enough.
I s'pose I've got to go the road I'm going:
Other folks have to, and why shouldn't I?
I almost think if I could do like you,
Drop everything and live out on the ground—
But it might be, some night, I shouldn't like it,
Or a long rain. I should soon get enough,
And be glad of a good roof overhead.
I've lain awake thinking of you, I'll warrant,
More than you have yourself, some of these nights.
The wonder was the tents weren't snatched away
From over you as you lay in your beds.
I haven't courage for a risk like that.
Bless you, of course, you're keeping me from work,
But the thing of it is, I need to *be* kept.
There's work enough to do—there's always that;
But behind's behind. The worst that you can do
Is set me back a little more behind.
I sha'n't catch up in this world, anyway.
I'd *rather* you'd not go unless you must.

In this monologue Frost manipulates a situation reminiscent of some of Browning's plots. A grim character sketch is created through the point of view of the main character herself; by implication, she gives us the action that precedes the immediate scene and projects its future certainty after this scene's end. Frost shows here his fondness for "queer" characters; for the almost half-sane, half-mad shell of a mind once bright and sensitive, now wavering on the border between acute awareness of fact and unconscious flight of fancy. The simple everyday language of the country woman is caught in Frost's handling of a loose iambic line. By ending sentences irregularly within the lines, Frost makes the flow of her monologue most natural. The syntax is never rearranged to fit any particular necessity of formal poetic rhythm; it is a *tour de force* of "man speaking" with the "sound of sense," and all within the confines of an unobtrusive metrical pattern. The blank verse monologue moves smoothly without stanza break, yet it suggests the erratic quality of the half-mad soliloquist as she pours forth her story. The scene is set by flashback in the conversation, and the action begins near the climax with a quick casual introduction typical of all of Frost's dramatic narratives.

The sad, mad woman—who need be neither sad nor mad except for circumstances beyond her own control—is interrupted suddenly in her

129

household chores which are never quite caught up. She is glad to move out of her kitchen confusion and to step outside to talk to the stranger. She admires the stranger from the outside world whose interest in their ferns is to her a remarkable reason for setting up a botanist's camp beside their lake. It is fantastic to her and rather beautiful too that for this man, "things like feathers" should dictate his "going and coming"; she compares this fantasy with her own strictly realistic approach to life. Her reasons for "going and coming" are much more serious and immediate, and yet she has no hope of any change at all. Most of Frost's dramatic monologues contain some such implied contrast of social and intellectual caste, one juxtaposed against the other for effect, with the author-listener merely transcribing for the reader who must make the transition philosophically. This poem's irony is maintained throughout in the very fact that here in the stranger the pitiful woman recognizes a willing ear, a sensitive kindred spirit, who loves even the frailest things of nature and who therefore may be expected to understand her own frailty. She has promised herself through the long wakeful nights to find this man, to seek him out for help and sympathy; but nothing seems to matter enough to expend the energy; and even if she found him, her natural reticence about her inabilities would make her uncommunicative. Now, having been found out herself, in her own yard, she is able to share her burdens with surprising spontaneity and to plunge into the telling of her bleak tale, "all gone wrong."

The conversational quality is maintained throughout; and as casually as the subject matter comes to the precarious mind, so is it brought forth without organization. Here Frost's "sound of sense" adopts the rambling vagaries of the woman's stream of *un*-consciousness and leaves the reader to interweave the all-too-apparent threads of madness and sanity. "You take the lake. . ." and her mind is off on tangents of fact and fancy in unbelievably pitiable confusion that is all too clear to the sympathetic ear. In her description of the lake we see her poetic instincts: she watches the storms with mingled delight and fright. . . "Drawing the slow waves whiter and whiter and whiter. . ." and the added iamb in this line offers the particular emphasis of the beauty and mystery in her mind. She can forget the household's drudgery if she can "take the dazzle" through her body in the sheer delight of the rising wind and waves. Yet whenever she attempts to be sure about anything else, the old refrain, "But I don't know. . ." is as far as her positive mind can contemplate or her positive action go. She is worn down by an inhuman quantity of work and a lack of human companionship. Her husband is as overworked as she; but he has more purpose and, also, her own love and help. The current hired hands and her husband are "the servants" who demand that she be *their* "servant" and never admit her dignity as a human being. And worse than the present is the terror of the past to haunt her in her future. She has become a mere mechanism no longer able to think coherently, feel sensitively, or act decisively about anything. And the horror is that she knows it, knows it for all its brutal, symptomatic fact; while she is equally sure that in other circumstances this would not have to be "the way through" for her.

This is a poem where the ironies of environment add to the tragedy of heredity. Frost's interest in nature's toll as well as its challenge (especially in the decadent back-country New England of his time) is well represented here. "Len thinks I'll be all right with doctoring. But it's not medicine. . . ." and the futility of any physical cure is as apparent to her as to the doctor himself. "Things over and over that just won't stay done" have become for her the constant maze that drives with precision to insanity. Len relies on physical strength and challenge; he urges her with dogged energy to see that "the best way out is always through." Her acceptance of this fact is a negative one—a last resort—and he cannot see the difference between his own approach and hers to life in general. This lack of skill, of sympathy, and of human understanding that has driven them both to this last resort is high-lighted by her remark, "And I agree to that, or in so far/ As that I can see no way out *but* through. . ./ . . . and then they'll be convinced." (This line represents one of Frost's favorite rhythmic devices in which he turns the strict metrical pattern to accent his "sound of sense" dialogue and actually uses the meter irregularly to advantage.)

She is as sure of her own doomed weakness as she is aware of her husband's living strength. The farmhands and road-workers who recognize the man's physical energy and mental inertia take advantage of him as they ignore her, and her only defense is to realize craftily that they might have reason to fear her own "queerness"—"there's two can play at that." But then, with this thought, the dread memory of her uncle's madness returns to haunt her half-sick, frightened mind and becomes more real in the telling than in the immediate present. Told with an awful calm, reviewed with each minute detail of horror, the whole terrible past incident of the aged lunatic is set against her own pitiable rationalization of her only "vacation" to the asylum where they have "every means proper." She quotes sentences and phrases from the people who have helped her make the rationalization and who have helped preserve the memory of the horror with the twanging bars of the cage still stored in the mind and the attic. . . "That was what marrying father meant to her," she recalls of her mother; and this is what marrying Len has meant to her. Both generations were equally devoted and equally devastated by forces that seem somehow uncontrollable in a world with too many physical absolutes to allow for mental deviations.

The line. . . "I've heard them say though/ They found a way to put a stop to it," is as punctiliously and casually final as the one in Browning's

"My Last Duchess" when "all smiles stopped together." And now the habit is so strong that she can imagine no other end than "taking her turn," though she once "looked to be happy and was" for a brief time. Len will not see, and she won't ask him; and even this re-telling has been only another wild rehearsal to fix in her mind the sure finalities. "I s'pose I've got to go the road I'm going. . . Other folks have to, and why shouldn't I?" And again she returns to the nearest finality of all— her immediate present—for the dramatic end. "Behind's behind. . ." and she picks up the dishcloth as the botanist departs with pity and terror in his mind. The last line, "I'd *rather* you'd not go unless you must. . ." is her final effort to move toward sanity, dignity, and communion.

This poem is representative of several which indicate Frost's interest in the psychology of basic human relations. Back-country stories of everyday decadence that in themselves seem provincial and prosaic are given a terrible highlight when shown in their stark loneliness against the rest of the "normal world." In the use of such psychological crises, he reaches a height of mastery seldom achieved in this dramatic poetic form.

THE WITCH OF COÖS

I stayed the night for shelter at a farm
Behind the mountain, with a mother and son,
Two old-believers. They did all the talking.

MOTHER. Folks think a witch who has familiar spirits
She could call up to pass a winter evening,
But won't, should be burned at the stake or something.
Summoning spirits isn't "Button, button,
Who's got the button," I would have them know.

SON. Mother can make a common table rear
And kick with two legs like an army mule.

MOTHER. And when I've done it, what good have I done?
Rather than tip a table for you, let me
Tell you what Ralle the Sioux Control once told me.
He said the dead had souls, but when I asked him
How could that be—I thought the dead were souls,
He broke my trance. Don't that make you suspicious
That there's something the dead are keeping back?
Yes, there's something the dead are keeping back.

SON. You wouldn't want to tell him what we have
Up attic, mother?

MOTHER. Bones—a skeleton.

SON. But the headboard of mother's bed is pushed
Against the attic door: the door is nailed.
It's harmless. Mother hears it in the night
Halting perplexed behind the barrier
Of door and headboard. Where it wants to get
Is back into the cellar where it came from.

MOTHER. We'll never let them, will we, son! We'll never!

SON. It left the cellar forty years ago
And carried itself like a pile of dishes
Up one flight from the cellar to the kitchen,
Another from the kitchen to the bedroom,
Another from the bedroom to the attic,
Right past both father and mother, and neither stopped it.
Father had gone upstairs; mother was downstairs.
I was a baby: I don't know where I was.

MOTHER. The only fault my husband found with me—
I went to sleep before I went to bed,
Especially in winter when the bed
Might just as well be ice and the clothes snow.
The night the bones came up the cellar-stairs
Toffile had gone to bed alone and left me,
But left an open door to cool the room off
So as to sort of turn me out of it.
I was just coming to myself enough
To wonder where the cold was coming from,
When I heard Toffile upstairs in the bedroom
And thought I heard him downstairs in the cellar.
The board we had laid down to walk dry-shod on
When there was water in the cellar in spring
Struck the hard cellar bottom. And then someone
Began the stairs, two footsteps for each step,
The way a man with one leg and a crutch,
Or a little child comes up. It wasn't Toffile;
It wasn't anyone who could be there.
The bulkhead double-doors were double-locked
And swollen tight and buried under snow.
The cellar windows were banked up with sawdust
And swollen tight and buried under snow.
It was the bones. I knew them—and good reason.
My first impulse was to get to the knob
And hold the door. But the bones didn't try
The door; they halted helpless on the landing,
Waiting for things to happen in their favor.
The faintest restless rustling ran all through them.
I never could have done the thing I did
If the wish hadn't been too strong in me

133

To see how they were mounted for this walk.
I had a vision of them put together
Not like a man, but like a chandelier.
So suddenly I flung the door wide on him.
A moment he stood balancing with emotion,
And all but lost himself. (A tongue of fire
Flashed out and licked along his upper teeth.
Smoke rolled inside the sockets of his eyes.)
Then he came at me with one hand outstretched,
The way he did in life once; but this time
I struck the hand off brittle on the floor,
And fell back from him on the floor myself.
The finger-pieces slid in all directions.
(Where did I see one of those pieces lately?
Hand me my button box—it must be there.)
I sat up on the floor and shouted, "Toffile,
It's coming up to you." It had its choice
Of the door to the cellar or the hall.
It took the hall door for the novelty,
And set off briskly for so slow a thing.
Still going every which way in the joints, though,
So that it looked like lightning or a scribble,
From the slap I had just now given its hand.
I listened till it almost climbed the stairs
From the hall to the only finished bedroom,
Before I got up to do anything;
Then ran and shouted, "Shut the bedroom door,
Toffile, for my sake!" "Company?" he said,
"Don't make me get up; I'm too warm in bed."
So lying forward weakly on the handrail
I pushed myself upstairs, and in the light
(The kitchen had been dark) I had to own
I could see nothing. "Toffile, I don't see it.
It's with us in the room though. It's the bones."
"What bones?" "The cellar bones—out of the grave."
That made him throw his bare legs out of bed
And sit up by me and take hold of me.
I wanted to put out the light and see
If I could see it, or else mow the room,
With our hands at the level of our knees,
And bring the chalk-pile down. "I'll tell you what—
It's looking for another door to try.
The uncommonly deep snow has made him think
Of his old song, *The Wild Colonial Boy,*
He always used to sing along the tote road.
He's after an open door to get outdoors.
Let's trap him with an open door up attic."
Toffile agreed to that, and sure enough,

Almost the moment he was given an opening,
The steps began to climb the attic stairs.
I heard them. Toffile didn't seem to hear them.
"Quick!" I slammed to the door and held the knob.
"Toffile, get nails." I made him nail the door shut
And push the headboard of the bed against it.
Then we asked was there anything
Up attic that we'd ever want again.
The attic was less to us than the cellar.
If the bones liked the attic, let them have it.
Let them stay in the attic. When they sometimes
Come down the stairs at night and stand perplexed
Behind the door and headboard of the bed,
Brushing their chalky skull with chalky fingers
With sounds like the dry rattling of a shutter,
That's when I sit up in the dark to say—
To no one any more since Toffile died.
Let them stay in the attic since they went there.
I promised Toffile to be cruel to them
For helping them be cruel once to him.

SON. We think they had a grave down in the cellar.

MOTHER. We know they had a grave down in the cellar.

SON. We never could find out whose bones they were.

MOTHER. Yes, we could too, son. Tell the truth for once.
They were a man's his father killed for me.
I mean a man he killed instead of me.
The least I could do was to help dig their grave.
We were about it one night in the cellar.
Son knows the story: but 'twas not for him
To tell the truth, suppose the time had come.
Son looks surprised to see me end a lie
We'd kept all these years between ourselves
So as to have it ready for outsiders.
But tonight I don't care enough to lie—
I don't remember why I ever cared.
Toffile, if he were here, I don't believe
Could tell you why he ever cared himself . . .

She hadn't found the finger-bone she wanted
Among the buttons poured out in her lap.
I verified the name next morning: Toffile.
The rural letter box said Toffile Lajway.

This best-known of Frost's dramatic narratives contains all the grim-
ness, passion, and sorrow of a classic Greek or Renaissance tragedy. Yet

135

it is related in the calm of a New England kitchen and is made all the more impressive from this perspective. The witch's reputation has been locally successful; she has summoned many spirits and is a careful guardian of the lore of her profession. The visitor who asks for shelter expects to hear only the common "old-believers'" tales of local hexes and spells as he drowses in the kitchen until the storm abates. "They did all the talking . . ." and suddenly he hears more of a local tragedy of blood than he would have ever dreamed possible from this quiet couple— the mad witch with her button box and her simple son, eager to protect his mother's reputation by keeping the family secret. The old woman on this stormy night suddenly questions her own worth as a witch, and for the first time she relates a tale from this world more terrible than any she could conjure from another—the tale of her own unfaithfulness and her own guilty payment for it through the years. She, more than anyone else, knows all too well that "there's something that the dead are keeping back"—and tonight she has lived too long. She no longer cares enough to conceal the fatal secret by the lie so well prepared and "ready for strangers."

Again Frost sets the stage with a receptive listener and the characters of the tragedy who naïvely tell all. The listener might well have been anyone who happened by on this particular evening when the elements and time all conspired to bring out the story. Frost merely suggests that this listener who evokes the story is sensitive enough to listen, learn, and be trusted. Even the son catches his responsiveness and suggests hopefully yet fearfully: "You wouldn't want to tell him?" So it is with an almost familial pride that these two, who have so long hoarded their secret, finally tell the tale of horror. The son, who has heard the story so often, knows it as well as his mother does. Like the mad woman in "A Servant to Servants," he too is well on his way to an insanity fostered by the environmental situation. He promises the stranger the security he has promised himself all these years: "It's harmless . . . and the door is nailed;" and the mother echoes as a constant refrain, "We'll never let them out, will we, son?" until he has been caught in league with her madness and hypnotized with guilt by association. "We'll never!" He knows the ghost so well that he even knows his parents' metaphors for its movements—"carried itself like a pile of dishes." He has inherited it all from his childhood, and the awful irony of his simple statement—"I don't know *where I* was" becomes dramatic for the sympathetic listener who hears him tell the tale too long remembered. His is a mere antiphonal response in his mother's ritual chant, and once he has introduced the theme and mood, she tells, unaided, a story of bloody deeds which happened so long ago that the neighborhood and the participants have forgotten why and care less.

Frost is careful to build the plot from the witch's point of view and to let her reveal in her telling the necessary symptoms of her own madness and guilt. She drops sufficient hints that the shared crime itself, as well as her original guilt behind it, have long since driven her to insanity. Her witch's facility is now an outward expression of the inner horror of her own spirit, and the crime is recalled in its entirety as her private nightmare. Here again Frost uses the successful technique of letting his plot unfold through a single point of view for heightened crisis—a technique in perspective used by all great dramatists and short story writers. It is all *her* story; Toffile never sees or hears the bones; Toffile merely goes along with his mad wife's hallucination, protectively doing whatever will calm her most quickly and acknowledging his own part in the horror that has come to her. She remembers in fantastically minute detail all of its sight and sound; the creak of the old board in the cellar (even why it was there); the lame, mounting step of the bones; and she is now suddenly smitten again with retrospective curiosity as to "how they were mounted . . . like a chandelier?" Her reason tells her over and over, and she has repeated it many times with the many tellings, that the doors and windows were all "swollen tight and buried under snow." This memory then is not from reason at all; it is from the spirit world to haunt her with her ancient curse. The actuality of the incident is complete in her memory to the slightest detail. One of the best examples of this visualization rhythmically and onomatopoetically is in the line in which the bones stand hesitant before the cellar door. "The faintest, restless rustling ran all through them. . ." (On the other hand, one finds here one of the few times when Frost departs from a diction appropriate to the character by having her say rather unexpectedly, "A moment he stood there balancing with emotion;" these last three words seem an expression too sophisticated for her.) Her witch's imagination is enough to provide additional tongues of fire and smoke for the ghostly eye sockets in the skull; her memory embellishes a good story beyond fact with emotion.

The ghost's hesitant gesture of either affection or anger is shattered by her blow, and the finger-bone properties for the drama—even now actually sought in the buttonbox as proof—serve as the listener's bridge with reality. This transition from fancy to fact grotesquely unifies the whole poem as it moves in the world of both reality and imagination. For the listener and the reader, the "Button-button" refrain at the start of the poem—which she scorns as the simplest sort of game and not *real* "witching"—is repeated in the search for the finger-bone button which she imagines or pretends she has brought from that wild night's events to the real world. The listener is able to depart after the story only daring to verify the name "Toffile" and is still wondering—though the buttons were never found—how much was the magic of her mind lost in memory and how much is grisly fact from the cellar grave. This quandary represents Frost's masterful use of one tiny detail to set the questioning double tone of the poem for reader and listener, and the reference is casual enough never to be obtrusively painful or inartistic. The coincidence of her asking for the button-box at the moment of the finger-bone incident in the tale heightens the immediate horror for the listener. Frost uses this technique for building suspense much as the Greek and Renaissance dramatists did. It poses the same interesting question of the identity of reality—whether it *be* fact or fancy—that the most modern psychological drama seeks to answer.

The dead husband recalled from her memory serves a purpose in plot, character, and tone. Toffile's sleepy response and rejection of "company" contrasts to her screaming summons—"for my sake," and the comic picture of his throwing his bare legs out of bed in horror is welcome relief and high contrast. The mental pictures of their mowing the room "to bring the chalk-pile down," or of their opening the door for the bones to ascend to the attic—all these to satisfy her frozen terror's desire to do something—anything—make the practical Toffile, who doesn't seem to hear or see, the ghastly living victim of the whole distorted crime itself. Her memory even supplies the motive for the ghost's restlessness, and she remembers from her youth this cheery, gay lover "who sang this song along the tote road." In her imagination, she sees his blithe vision in contrast to the stodgy Toffile, who goes to bed early and dreams no guilty dreams. Such a memory enlightens the tale's telling and recreates her own sense of guilt. The sheer relief of the too short line, "Then we asked was there anything. . . ." is reflected in its purposeful broken rhythm as Frost makes his form reveal its own content in "the sound of sense." In the impulsive pauses for breath and sanity, Frost's fine use of speech meters matches his ideas with *ir*regularity when necessary. Few lines in Senecan drama can match the stark sense impressions of the bones—"brushing their chalky skull with chalky fingers/ With sounds like the dry rattling of a shutter"! There is self-conscious terror in the old lady's finality, now that she is left without the grim, loving protection of old Toffile: "If the bones liked the attic, let them have it. . ./ Let them stay in the attic since they went there."

Her confession comes quite naïvely and casually as she muses the story and keeps her promise to the dead Toffile to "be cruel to them/ For helping them be cruel to him once." At this particular high point of drama, the son's interruption comes as a break back to reality and is especially important for the manner in which syntax—"man speaking"— reveals the whole story's crisis. The contrasting parallels of "think" and "know" between his careful sentences and her devastatingly final one bring the plot to its peak of intensity. Here is a recognition scene in two short lines. After this, the dénouement comes with swift, sure clarity. "The least I could do was help dig the grave. . ./ Son looks surprised to see me end the lie." Toffile himself, after all these years with the weight of the burden, might even ask himself as she does on this night "why he ever cared." But the bitter irony of love lost in its own gaining is still to be lamented. The stranger, after a night of witch's tale of truth-far-stranger-than-fiction, goes his way in the morning with one of Frost's typical fast finales with reality regained as he stops only to verify the family name. "What's in a name?" . . . ; it can only be observed, remembered, and perhaps forgotten with the shadowy tale best left undisturbed.

The conciseness and precision of this tale, the graceful suggestion, and the humor make the horror all the more poignant; the magic of this simple telling is far more impressive than any table-tipping or summoning of spirits. The reader is left with the old rhyme haunting him: "Button, button, who's got the button?"

HOME BURIAL

He saw her from the bottom of the stairs
Before she saw him. She was starting down,
Looking back over her shoulder at some fear.
She took a doubtful step and then undid it
To raise herself and look again. He spoke
Advancing toward her: 'What is it you see
From up there always—for I want to know.'
She turned and sank upon her skirts at that,
And her face changed from terrified to dull.
He said to gain time: 'What is it you see,'
Mounting until she cowered under him.
'I will find out now—you must tell me, dear.'

She, in her place, refused him any help
With the least stiffening of her neck and silence.
She let him look, sure that he wouldn't see,
Blind creature and awhile he didn't see.
But at last he murmured, 'Oh,' and again, 'Oh.'

'What is it—what?' she said.

                                    'Just that I see.'

'You don't,' she challenged. 'Tell me what it is.'

'The wonder is I didn't see at once.
I never noticed it from here before.
I must be wonted to it—that's the reason.
The little graveyard where my people are!
So small the window frames the whole of it.

139

Not so much larger than a bedroom, is it?
There are three stones of slate and one of marble,
Broad-shouldered little slabs there in the sunlight
On the sidehill. We haven't to mind *those*.
But I understand: it is not the stones,
But the child's mound—'

               'Don't, don't, don't, don't,' she cried—.

She withdrew shrinking from beneath his arm
That rested on the bannister, and slid downstairs;
And turned on him with such a daunting look,
He said twice over before he knew himself:
'Can't a man speak of his own child he's lost?'

'Not you! Oh, where's my hat? Oh, I don't need it!
I must get out of here. I must get air.
I don't know rightly whether any man can.'

'Amy! Don't go to someone else this time.
Listen to me. I won't come down the stairs.'
He sat and fixed his chin between his fists.
'There's something I should like to ask you, dear.'

'You don't know how to ask it.'

                    'Help me, then.'

Her fingers moved the latch for all reply.

'My words are nearly always an offense.
I don't know how to speak of anything
So as to please you. But I might be taught
I should suppose. I can't say I see how.
A man must partly give up being a man
With women-folk. We could have some arrangement
By which I'd bind myself to keep hands off
Anything special you're a-mind to name.
Though I don't like such things 'twixt those that love.
Two that don't love can't live together without them.
But two that do can't live together with them.'
She moved the latch a little. 'Don't—don't go.
Don't carry it to someone else this time.
Tell me about it if it's something human.
Let me into your grief. I'm not so much
Unlike other folks as your standing there
Apart would make me out. Give me my chance.
I do think, though, you overdo it a little.
What was it brought you up to think it the thing
To take your mother-loss of a first child
So inconsolably—in the face of love.
You'd think his memory might be satisfied—'

'There you go sneering now!'

                           'I'm not, I'm not!
You make me angry. I'll come down to you.
God, what a woman! And it's come to this,
A man can't speak of his own child that's dead.'

'You can't because you don't know how to speak.
If you had any feelings, you that dug
With your own hand—how could you?—his little grave;
I saw you from that very window there,
Making the gravel leap and leap in air,
Leap up, like that, like that, and land so lightly
And roll back down the mound beside the hole.
I thought, Who is that man? I didn't know you.
And I crept down the stairs and up the stairs
To look again, and still your spade kept lifting.
Then you came in. I heard your rumbling voice
Out in the kitchen, and I don't know why,
But I went near to see with my own eyes.
You could sit there with the stains on your shoes
Of the fresh earth from your own baby's grave
And talk about your everyday concerns.
You had stood the spade up against the wall
Outside there in the entry, for I saw it.'

'I shall laugh the worst laugh I ever laughed.
I'm cursed, God, if I don't believe I'm cursed.'

'I can repeat the very words you were saying.
"Three foggy mornings and one rainy day
Will rot the best birch fence a man can build."
Think of it, talk like that at such a time!
What had how long it takes a birch to rot
To do with what was in the darkened parlor.
You *couldn't* care! The nearest friends can go
With anyone to death, comes so far short
They might as well not try to go at all.
No, from the time when one is sick to death,
One is alone, and he dies more alone.
Friends make pretense of following to the grave,
But before one is in it, their minds are turned
And making the best of their way back to life
And living people, and things they understand.
But the world's evil. I won't have grief so
If I can change it. Oh, I won't, I won't!'

'There, you have said it all and you feel better.
You won't go now. You're crying. Close the door.
The heart's gone out of it: why keep it up.
Amy! There's someone coming down the road!'

141

'*You*—oh, you think the talk is all. I must go—
Somewhere out of this house. How can I make you—'

'If—you—do!' She was opening the door wider.
'Where do you mean to go? First tell me that.
I'll follow and bring you back by force. I *will!*—'

Frost has often been praised for his sensitive portrayals of women, and these last two dramatic narratives show great understanding of feminine psychology. They also show his understanding of the "masculine mind" as it copes with female personality. Here again he manages the cadences of colloquial speech in blank verse from which he deviates only for accent of crisis or irony. The writer sets the stage here with a production director's finesse: the tragic woman imperiously high up on the stairs, stage-center; her misunderstood and misunderstanding husband below, looking up as she starts hesitantly down. The conversation needs only her one uncertain motion for introduction to the tenseness of the scene. Such uses of stage directions through gestures, telling looks, vocabulary of movement ("cowering," "mounting," "stiffening," "advancing," "sinking") all fit adroitly into the poetic pattern and are unobtrusively a part of the fabric of the dramatic narrative. They help tell the story visually without the usual parenthesis of the dramatist's orders. It is not even necessary here to add speech tags, because inflection and diction identify the speakers sufficiently.

When the husband, distraught with worry and aware of his own futile efforts to understand, finally catches his wife in this gesture of departure down the stairs, he impulsively risks a showdown with her silent condemnation that has judged him for so long. His is the practical healthy attitude of a man living a full life close to the soil, able to take either joy or sorrow with equal stature and to recoup his energies and forces without the scars of extravagant emotional tensions. His is a generous spirit, eager to please; if less sensitive than hers, at least more loving and unselfish in an overt and forgiving way. "Blind creature" that he is to the fatal window, he sees farther *beyond* the window into life than she does. "But at last he murmured 'Oh,' and again 'Oh!' " and finally recognizing the sight of the small grave, he tries to accept her grief as added burden for his own. He excuses himself—"I must be wonted to it"—and yet the little graveyard holds no terror for him; only security as the last resting place for "my people," no larger than a bedroom, just as practical, just as necessary, yet just as temporary for sleeping a last finite sleep. Even the tombstones of slate and marble suggest not death to him, but rather a stable record of continuing generations well lived, now peacefully dead. They are actually landmarks toward the future with a very

142

natural progression that he feels instinctively once the first shock of death is over.

But it is the child's recent mound that evokes her wild tirade of grief, and he realizes too late that he has insensitively misunderstood her own resentment of *him* in her grief for the child recently buried. Suddenly it becomes not the tragedy of the child, but his own tragedy, her love lost but somehow still living to haunt him here. He stands frustrated on the stairs unable to reach or to help her, and he muses pathetically, "I don't rightly know whether any man can. . ." as he feels the distance between their points of view widen. She maintains a curiously haughty Victorian attitude toward his masculine insensitivity, and she wounds his pride by doubting his very sanity which is too rational for her to endure. He pleads for her help, acknowledging his usual offense to her and asks to be taught. His humility is long-suffering, and he knows that he has blundered many times before this one. The words, "I can't say I see *how*. . ." are important, however, for his natural dignity; he is willing to give up a part of his masculine prerogative to meet an adversary, even death, face-to-face, man-to-man. But he wonders why "a man must partly give up being a man with womenfolk. . ." Finally, why must the tragedy of one child lost seem so final as to demand her rejection of all future children who might logically be expected to comfort a healthy grief eventually? Here are prototypes of every strong man regretting and somehow resenting every frail woman. And his is the larger sense and sensibility, the greater wisdom when he regrets his own promised reticences:

> Though I don't like such things 'twixt those that love.
> Two that don't love can't live together without them,
> And two that do can't live together with them.

His plea to be let into her grief is met with her high irony. How can such an insensitive person as he ever realize her depth of grief or hope to share it? And ironically her grief seems to come more from his error than from the child's death. When he finally realizes what the insult is, the most terrible lines of this desperate man rise in masculine wrath from his lips:

> I shall laugh the worst laugh I ever laughed.
> I'm cursed, God, if I don't believe I'm cursed.

The fact of his labor in digging the grave had been the one reality that he could contribute in entrusting their child—as much beloved and lamented by him as by her—to nature's good offices. With the tragedy of death done, any potential recreation for him can only come as lives are now resumed and death-in-life is supplanted by life-in-death as the pattern is carried forward. His actual physical digging had been done with the usual force that comes of long experience in finding surcease from grief and trouble in hard work, in hand work that softens heartaches. She cannot see this. The fact that his spade could leap and leap and turn over with its usual dexterity a carefully piled little grave is for her a pure desecration of the love that once created the child and now buries it. Her elegiac wail that "the nearest anyone can go with anyone to death is too far short" has all the awful wisdom of acute and sudden grief and all the desolate loneliness of one who has met the problem for the first time. But his is the wiser grief that, having stared straight into the abyss, is now capable of an overt action that will lift him out of it again. Hers is a masochistic, selfish upbraiding of the world itself, a refusal to let the burden of grief be allayed by any trite or hackneyed continuity for condolence. "Wail, for the world's wrong." "The times are out of joint." She joins the classic chorus of all who wail thus: :'I won't have grief so if I can change it.' (Frost uses his meters here with skill in irregularity for emphasis of tone.) She ruefully rejects any assurance from her husband that the worst is over. He has even made the crude statement about rotting birches while their child's corpse lay unburied in the darkened parlor, an unforgivable crudity! She cannot or will not understand that he seeks the tiny, pitiful reassurances of everyday life, if only by casual conversation, by trite aphorism, to mend the deep grief for both of them. She assumes the cosmic responsibility of channelling both of their griefs to her own set pattern. His recognition of her hysteria, of her perverted sorrow, of her exaggerated pleas for solitude faces the futility of the half-hearted threats that she may never have the real courage to carry out. She fumbles with the latch; she opens the door wider; she hunts her hat; and finally he resorts to a very healthy rage and the threat of force to bring her mind to focus. Sympathy, so insulted as his own has been, can be strained just so far. The final indignity of all would be for a stranger to see her leaving the house now. He resents any public knowledge of this lack of understanding between them in this crisis. "Someone coming down the road" can either save them from the final break or drive her out forever.

The poet does not say whether the husband's vow to find his wife and return her impels her to flee or keeps her from going. His is the quicker, more impulsive reaction, the more positive one, and the one that can best restore them both to an objective sanity. The drama ends on a high emotional peak; the curtains are closed quickly without Frost's returning his reader to his own world. The reader is left to complete the tale.

The characteristic "sound of sense" is created throughout by the use of broken-line dialogue, conversational elisions, and colloquial references. These set in the highly emotional situation make for one of Frost's most effective syntheses of content, form, and mood.

144

Chapter Ten

Satires

DEPARTMENTAL

An ant on the tablecloth
Ran into a dormant moth
Of many times his size.
He showed not the least surprise.
His business wasn't with such.
He gave it scarcely a touch,
And was off on his duty run.
Yet if he encountered one
Of the hive's enquiry squad
Whose work is to find out God
And the nature of time and space,
He would put him onto the case.
Ants are a curious race;
One crossing with hurried tread
The body of one of their dead
Isn't given a moment's arrest—
Seems not even impressed.
But he no doubt reports to any
With whom he crosses antennae,
And they no doubt report
To the higher up at court.
Then word goes forth in Formic:
'Death's come to Jerry McCormic,
Our selfless forager Jerry.
Will the special Janizary
Whose office it is to bury
The dead of the commissary
Go bring him home to his people.
Lay him in state on a sepal.
Wrap him for shroud in a petal.
Embalm him with ichor of nettle.
This is the word of your Queen.'

And presently on the scene
Appears a solemn mortician;
And taking formal position
With feelers calmly atwiddle,
Seizes the dead by the middle,
And heaving him high in the air,
Carries him out of there.
No one stands round to stare.
It is nobody else's affair.

It couldn't be called ungentle.
But how thoroughly departmental.

This example of Frost's satiric animal fables marches with tongue-in-cheek glibness and flippancy by means of its three-beat couplets rhymed with a sort of Ogden Nash facility. Frost has called it "my heavy-duty poem" because of the intensive hammering beat of the rhythm, and this emphasis highlights the comic seriousness of the situation and idea. The very short lines and the tricky rhyming of the couplets ("any"—"antennae") add to the farcical, burlesque effect. Yet the poet is deadly serious in his implied commentary that men, like ants, are a "curious race." For added emphasis, this theme statement is the only one that breaks the rhyme and so stands above and outside any couplet.

The man stands over the tablecloth and amusedly watches the apparently insensitive ant beneath him, a black speck on the vast white. This duty-bound little insect, whose only function or interest is to do his own restricted job, never questions his status. Meeting curious interferences, he shows neither fear, amazement, nor interest. "His business wasn't with such"; so he goes off to his duty for the day. And Frost feels a twinge of remorse for all the similar human ants who run off, day after day, to little private duties by commuter train or automobile with hardly a look at the curious totality of the world around them. If his ant happens to run into one of the enquiry squad whose work happens to be the investigation of God, time, and space, his duty is to report the miracle and leave the investigation up to the proper specialists. Safe within their own Institute for Higher Ant Learning, these specialists may figure out on a blackboard what the everyday ant has just encountered in his own pathway. The ordinary ant is not to think for himself, to wonder, or to reason, except within the limited field of his own particular duty. "Ants are a curious race," Frost says; there are no amateur grassroots philosophers among them—only professionals. The reader is left to explicate the ironic analogy at his own human level.

Unimpressed by the strangeness of the huge dormant moth, this ant is equally unimpressed by the strangeness of the little dead ant like himself.

146

Neither phenomenon bothers his small closed mind. He sees no relation between this death and his own potential end—no reason for it to be either welcomed or avoided. Death is only a quantitative statistic to be calculated in the feeding of the race. The satire of bureaucracy goes on as Frost sets the rhythm to work for him in the lines, "And he *no* doubt reports to any/ With whom *he* crosses antennae/ *And they* no doubt report/ To the *higher* up at court." Magnificent Swiftian elements are here as the word goes out "in Formic" and the corpse of Jerry McCormic, "our selfless forager," is attended by the special mortician for the commissary workers. This is the land of "Big Brother" where even morticians are graded and appointed to certain areas of practice; where creative Promethean man is lost in the welter of adding machines, official communiques, and reports. Not even death itself is sufficiently impressive and personal to stop the eternal foraging. Selfless Jerry's corpse is mechanically hoisted into position by the proper mortician and given the rites proper to his class; a sepal as bier, a petal for grave clothes, and ichor-of-nettle embalming fluid. The insensitivity of human burial rituals is given an ironic emphasis by the phrase "feelers calmly atwiddle" and the words "middle" and "heaving." But in this world of ants, no one stands round to stare or find this incongruous. The mortician is as dignified and as duty-bound as the rest; he too is a forager dedicated to his own area of industry. This too is taken for granted, and he proceeds with his work without audience. In such a controlled society one individual more or less is of little personal concern to the entire collective economy.

How reasonable it is, Frost seems to say slyly, and yet how terribly insensitive. But who is man to scoff at the ant world? Man with his superior endowments doesn't stop to stare and wonder at his own relation to God, time, and space when he meets them in his own backyard; but he does stare with shock and curiosity when the cortege of one of his own marches through his life. How much better to stare and wonder before . . . before "it is nobody's else's affair." To departmentalize death, Frost is saying, in part, is to ignore it; to departmentalize life is also to ignore it. All values are lost in such indignity. "The word goes forth in Formic" as a mechanical, generalized announcement in the typically "ant" world; Frost would have it go forth in the sensitive "human" world in a spiritually individualized fashion. The poet stands off from the poem for a brief pause at the break before the crushing couplet in which he neatly levels bureaucracy, socialism, mass education, etc., with all their little subdivisions of stupidity—all in one stroke of creative genius. The message has been literally pounded out; the artist's rhythm and images have spoken the devastatingly final blow:

> It couldn't be called ungentle,
> But how thoroughly departmental.

The people along the sand
All turn and look one way.
They turn their back on the land.
They look at the sea all day.

As long as it takes to pass
A ship keeps raising its hull;
The wetter ground like glass
Reflects a standing gull.

The land may vary more;
But wherever the truth may be—
The water comes ashore,
And the people look at the sea.

They cannot look out far.
They cannot look in deep.
But when was that ever a bar
To any watch they keep?

This is one of Frost's most significant commentaries on *genus homo*: his calm, flat statement of the wondrous yet simple curiosity that makes man continue to look out from his life and wonder. The brief poetic essay asserts that it is the particular dignity of man to search beyond the knowable—his obvious simple duty as human from which he cannot and will not escape. The form of the poem is as simple as its idea: the diction is almost monosyllabic; the images are all simple objects, one of everything against a flat, black sea and sky. "The people" are the only plurals, and even they seem small, isolated individuals as they stand forever looking beyond their own known limits. Yet their common turning to look one way, in the quiet gesture of obedience to something instinctive within them, joins them into one great singular entity again; and they are drawn as tides are drawn, inexorably as many waves move in one vast motion. The tone of the poem is as calm and final as the waters they watch; short declarative sentences end in periods one after another. The repetition of "they turn. . . they look. . . they cannot. . . they cannot. . ." eventually becomes a rhythmic chant that gives their motion in the mind's image the precision of dancers' choreography, and they seem directed as automatons or puppets.

And yet the very concept of the poem is the disproving of this automatic hypnosis. The logical turn would be *toward* land where life and living make the scene more interesting, more vital, more curious for the watchful eye. The people, it would seem, would naturally prefer this landscape's merry-go-round of events where locomotion is faster and action is gayer. Why then, do the people come to the sea for surcease; why do they flock in wonder to the water as a source of salvation? What is there in its unknown calm depth that lures them away from the known, the understood, the regular, and the controlled? "They turn their back to the land/ They look at the sea all day." The sea can offer only a few signs of life—the transience of a single ship that raises its hull only momentarily and then disappears mysteriously again into the depths behind the same horizon over which it rose. A single gull stands poised for flight against the wet sand which reflects its distorted image in the half-water, half-land boundary of the shore. "The people" themselves become a single entity in their common watch beside the water. All the images are single, reduced to one specimen, yet generically complete and representative. Their movements are slow-motion gestures of primal motivation, as poised and irrevocable as those of a formal ballet of life.

These three images are all the poet paints in the seascape except for the endless water and the waving motion of its backdrop. Yet the peoeple—"The People"—generically and individually turn to watch, to be forever fascinated by the inexplicable, even though a more ordered life continues behind them on the land. This is Melville's sea—"the fathoms of Abraham"—and here, as in *Moby Dick,* it demands the natural return for man, the resumption of his native, primitive state, the proper acknowledgement of his protozoic genesis. Though he has crawled ashore, the endless waters of the world still attract him. They are no longer a habitat but an enemy to be distrusted; yet they are still enchanting, and he feels somehow "at home" watching them. They are really his conqueror to be withstood, but they are alluringly attractive; he continues to look blindly and blandly, seeing really nothing. His search may be to his credit or his discredit; Frost is careful to reserve judgment for his reader's own interpretation. Stupidity or apathy may shut man's eyes to the possible things behind him on land from which he would profit more. He is certainly not using reason when he stands and stares at the flat water; the allure is something deeper than the merely rational mind can analyze.

Frost once said that the first line of the third stanza originally read, "Some say the land has more," rather than "The land may vary more." So the eventual revision took out even the slightly personal element of the "some" and left no human observation, simply potential fact—"The land *may* vary more" and "wherever the truth may be. . ." leave the subjunctive doubt. The poet says nothing *for sure* in this poem except that the people look "neither out far nor in deep." Is he playing a poetic joke, ironically satirizing man's curiosity which for him is no more than the waving antennae of the insect world? Or is he remarking on the questing spirit of *genus homo* that makes him forever dissatisfied with his present habitat and forces him to plumb the depths of the ocean and to stare into interstellar space? And given such an urge, what does he expect to see, and how will he know it when and if he does see it? Rejecting the ship and the gull as mundane and recognizable—man-made and God-made—what else is there left to see in the sea? Why is the watch kept and for whom? Is it mere self-satisfaction in an amoral diligence without plan? Or is there an almost magical control through faith that drives man never to give up the searching eye, the listening ear, and always to turn his back to the land? These are the complicated rhetorical questions that the simple poetic lines evoke in the reader's mind when he fully absorbs the images.

The poet knows three things for certain: the people will continue to look; they cannot look out far; they cannot look in deep. He allows himself only one brief and dignified justification of himself as one of "The People." He does not even say "we"; but he joins forces with the rest of the human race when he climaxes the deceptively flat, calm poem with a grandiose, dignified ascent at its end: "But when was that ever a bar/ To any watch they keep?" The final question holds very subtle persuasion—flattery for the human reader from one of the most unobtrusive yet one of the most human of poets. These little men, who on the poetic seascape's low shore have seemed only dots against the sky and water, are looking constantly with their myopic eyes turned out through the gathering gloom beyond the mere reflections of their known world for more than the seeable, for more, no doubt, than is really knowable. Stark simplicity gives them and the poem common dignity.

The metrical pattern of the poem echoes its calm, flat quality of image. Frost catches the monotony of the message in his rhythmic beat. He keeps the major accents in the same place in every line (an unusual regularity for him)—on the second and last beats. There is only one significant variation, and it is appropriately in the most significant line on the most important word: "But wherever the *truth* may be. . ." Each line seems to flow directly into the next as though they were all in the sequence of the most unruffled prose statement. Any elisions are kept even and simple. The sentences are all flat declarations, often spoken almost entirely in monosyllables. The entire poem seems to be a well-organized essay paragraph except for its insistent metrical beat. At the very end the poet alerts the lulled reader to poetry again by two short sentences that repeat the theme as they announce the final stanza; the climax comes quickly with the direct, proud rhetorical question at the end. The answer is obvious.

HAPPINESS MAKES UP IN HEIGHT
FOR WHAT IT LACKS IN LENGTH

Oh, stormy stormy world.
The days you were not swirled
Around with mist and cloud,
Or wrapped as in a shroud,
And the sun's brilliant ball
Was not in part or all
Obscured from mortal view—
Were days so very few
I can but wonder whence
I get the lasting sense
Of so much warmth and light.
If my mistrust is right
It may be altogether
From one day's perfect weather,
When starting clear at dawn,
The day swept clearly on
To finish clear at eve.
I verily believe
My fair impression may
Be all from that one day
No shadow crossed but ours
As through its blazing flowers
We went from house to wood
For change of solitude.

The form of this poem is one of Frost's favorites. With remarkable virtuosity he uses three-stress couplets for a twenty-four line poem in which there are only three sentences. The short lines keep the pace breathless and the mood ecstatic and are therefore functionally related to the poem's joyous idea. The mood moves from the depths of a gloomy storm to the brilliance of love in solitude. Structurally the poem is like a pyramid. Onomatopoetically the alliterative sounds of "s" in the first four lines develop the constant, lasting storm; and suddenly out of it explodes the "brilliant ball" of the sun with the two "b" sounds to accent and point the exclamation of light. The one day's perfect clarity is described by the one happy verb "swept" with all its motion and light and firmness—"clear at dawn" to "clear at eve"—and the parallels are carefully balanced and developed.

The pattern of invocation, of direct address at the beginning briefly marks a kind of submission to all the necessary storms to be endured during the majority of days, years, and lifetimes left after this one day of glory. Here is rational man thinking—statistical man who makes weather

151

maps and charts and realizes that his sun actually shines much less than it is hidden and that all his success with prediction may be thwarted by a sudden freak wind. Hence this scientific man should prepare himself for gloom and make the best of it to shelter his body and mind and feelings while he realizes that it may be his fate to have much more of gloom than less of it. Yet suddenly, (as though the vision had finally come from the watch kept in the last poem discussed) one assurance of the sun through the entirety of one perfect day can somehow make up in height for the longest length of gloom. True, it must be one *perfect* day, the one that sweeps clear from dawn to eve to make the difference. Thinking man will not be lured to satisfaction by any half-way grey substitutes. Skeptical man must have real perfection at least *once* to set the pattern for it again; he will not be compromised with anything less than perfection. Yet why this fair impression of "mistrust" at all, the poet muses. How can the one against the many make so *much* difference to change him from the steady, rational pessimist of all dark days into the flaunting, ecstatic optimist of this one short day's delight? Is man to throw away all his caution for the ironic teasing of a universal power who allows so few perfections to set off unmercifully the all-too-frequent imperfections? Or is he to seize upon the few perfections and be happily satisfied to indulge without question? In the single image Frost combines the essential philosophical questions of *The Rubaiyat, Job,* and *The Psalms,* and he hints at a kind of existential resolution.

The poet's own perfect day was a day shared in a love that elevated *it* above all other clear days *without* love and left its essence glowing in his memory forever. *"My* fair impression" acknowledges as climax that fact that it was *"our* day" when "no shadow crossed but ours." Man reaches his highest potential for joy only with a shared ecstasy of communion that is all the more satisfying because he has known the many undesigned terrors of the individual desert places and even of the lovely, dark deep woods. On one such perfect day, the blazing flowers reflect the love again which knows its own sufficient solitude yet paradoxically needs and seeks the magnitude of the entire world in which to compass it. As such, the poem's "message" reflects one of Frost's most optimistic moods.

And yet the phrase "change of solitude" casts a brief Frostian shadow of transience over the perfection of the end. In spite of this, the poet has been willing to spend all the years of gloom for this one day of sheer delight. Nor does he stand resentfully counting the gloom away until the light shall come again. Here is a robustness, a healthy psyche that admits its *"mis*trust may be right" at times—at least right enough to measure happiness in height rather than in the usual length of the world's rule. This is the same mind that can note such perfection of design in this one day for himself and at the same time fear the defection of design for others less fortunate in another poem. Any series of Frost's poems shows the obvious error in drawing philosophical conclusions too rigidly from a single or even a dozen representative poems. The poet is still the man with the changeable mind and therefore the man with the sane mind.

Here is man willing on this one day to luxuriate in his own physical perfection of nature itself. Why spoil it with the backlog of past trouble and gloom or the foretaste of horror to follow if it will? He is willing to take advantage of the moment to acknowledge "*mis*trust" in it and not begrudge its source by contrast. But he is also willing to exist in its essence for its own sake and to savor it. As in all of Frost's love poetry, the touch is light with the emphasis always on incident rather than emotion. And it is a quiet reminder that a deep and lasting love in his life has had a good deal to do with his poetry and philosophy. This one poem is representative of his many simple yet sensitive tributes to that love.

CHOOSE SOMETHING LIKE A STAR

O Star (the fairest one in sight),
We grant your loftiness the right
To some obscurity of cloud—
It will not do to say of night,
Since dark is what brings out your light.
Some mystery becomes the proud.
But to be wholly taciturn
In your reserve is not allowed.
Say something to us we can learn
By heart and when alone repeat.
Say something! And it says, 'I burn.'
But say with what degree of heat.
Talk Fahrenheit, talk Centigrade.
Use language we can comprehend.
Tell us what elements you blend.
It gives us strangely little aid,
But does tell something in the end.
And steadfast as Keats' Eremite,
Not even stooping from its sphere,
It asks a little of us here.
It asks of us a certain height,
So when at times the mob is swayed
To carry praise or blame too far,
We may choose something like a star
To stay our minds on and be staid.

This last poem has been chosen from the *Complete Poems* of Frost in a section that he calls an "Afterword." Here is the poet ripe with years, still full of the same old questions, slightly tired, almost impatient with a universe that still refuses the answer he has sought so long. This is the normal petulance of any serious, dignified seeker who has suddenly been forced to throw away his usual polite reserve in the haste of time's sudden pace and who must now admit, after all, that his human anguish to know is still as great an irritant as ever. He is still willing to seek answers not of any common star, but rather with proper deference to address the "fairest one in sight." Stars have long been the favorite place for Frost to look when the dark woods' temptation becomes too great. He is willing to grant this "fairest one in sight" its proper proud obscurity to the mind of small, insignificant, questioning man. He knows that the vision will not clear easily, that the answer will not be sudden—that it will be, as usual, relative to "the fun in how you say a thing." More irregular in rhyme than the usual Frost pattern, this poem is full of interesting reversals; and these purposefully carry the thought beyond the mere sing-song danger of the four-beat verse. It reveals a sort of modified, enlarged sonnet form in the manner with which thought and structure are coordinated by careful planning.

Man admires the very mystery of the star and is enchanted the more by the great contrast of background that sets off its brilliance. It demands deference, but man's reasoning mind drives him to inquire directly, and he resents its complete silence. Man demands as his right, *some* answer. He stands below—eons of time and space below—and shouts in his infinitesimal voice, "Say something!" He even plans to shoot himself toward it to catch its answer as soon as he can manage it scientifically. Its silence enrages and captivates him. With magnificent parallelism of structure within the same line, the star answers with the all-enveloping declaration of its own cosmic existence, "I burn." The star's declaration of its simplicity *and* its complexity is temptation for the seeker. "Tell more," call the scientist and the priest; "Use language we can understand," calls the poet: language of textbook, laboratory, or fable. "Tell us what elements you blend," whether they be those of atomic chart or mystery ritual.

The poet struggles to the last period of "in the end" and lets his irregular rhyme evoke the struggle for the reader. He finally arrives at one satisfaction: not the satisfaction of fact, but one of interpretation. What is it that "it *does* tell" in the end? Only when the man stops shouting in defiant challenge and steps back to listen to the silence, to feel the omnipresent burning, does he realize what the star does tell. Actually, he learns that the answer is not a "telling" at all, but an "asking." The last message comes with all the dignity and religious majesty of the

154

"bright Star" that was Keats' "Eremite"; this star is as faithful as was that dedicated recluse of the heavens—"not even stooping from its sphere" to announce the message. With no condescension, "It asks a little of us here." The important words are "little" and "here." All that *can* be understood "here" *is* a very "little"; and the interstellar spaces are too far to be bridged by more for our time. What is the "little" that it asks? A looking up, "a certain height" for the stature of man. It asks respectful recognition of its own distance, its own inspiration beyond the mundane, lower, mob-swayed planets who may mistake praise or blame. But there is no mistaking this star. It is too far removed for man's margin for error; it is too certain in its very remoteness; it is happily inaccessible except by wonder and perspective and peace. To observe it, then, is man's happy, proud privilege. The poem's finale is in the same conversational "sound of sense" that characterized its dialogue from the start:

> We may choose something like a star
> To stay our minds on and be staid.

Conclusion

"I would have written of me on my stone:
I had a lover's quarrel with the world."
—"The Lesson for Today"

At eighty-eight years of age Robert Frost is still summarizing his career with one more poem, prose epitaph, or epigram that he regards affectionately as his last expression. It is hard for him to anticipate "the end of a season," and yet he knows that it is impossible to escape it. (He remarked to this writer in 1959, "Hurry with the book so I can read it too!") His active mind keeps adding codicils of wisdom to the literary heritage published as *Complete Poems* in 1949. This volume ended with a postscript section called "An Afterword"; this section's last poem is called "Closed for Good" after an original finale entitled "To the Right Person." In 1954 he published "One More Brevity" in a periodical, and in 1959 he brought out a volume of children's poems still enticingly titled "You Come Too."

In spite of the fact that Frost's poetic career finally seems to be reaching conclusion, there is as yet little good criticism of his work; there is too much eulogy by admiring friends and too much antipathy by critics of the "new poetry's" school. Frost is admittedly full of some recognizable wisdom for his many readers; he has an audience such as few modern poets have, and his readers are constantly comforted whether they skim or read deeply. Actually his poetry is far too close and tight to encourage many superficial disciples either as readers or writers. Yet he has offered as much to as many people as any poet of our time, and he has had a rather remarkable effect on those who either understand or misunderstand him.

In content, he is a poet of nature and of man in nature, but not traditionally so. His forms represent basically the skillful use of regular patterns of meter and poetic devices, but they are often subjected to and enhanced by a whimsical variation of rhythm and rhyme that makes his own particular "sound of sense." When he seems to be telling a simple parable or creating a casual rustic drama, he may actually be exploring a subtle philosophical point through the use of a muted symbolism. Though his narrative poetry may seem to the casual reader

156

as logical, realistic, and sensible as a Hemingway story, it may be analyzed by the careful reader—as may the Hemingway—to reveal complex levels of meaning between the apparently stark lines.

In watching the development of this admittedly "original 'ordinary' man,"[1] critics find him in his old age lamenting the same griefs and savoring the same joys that he had experienced as a young poet. Still "sure that all he thought was true," he acknowledges misgivings but knows that he can "maintain the quest." As a poet, he has had to write tragedy if he would see life whole, but the constant balance between cheer and gloom has been for him a salutary thing. His play of mind between these two seems to have been the major key to Frost's career as man and poet.

As a relativist then, he is a poet of tolerance, quite unlike his fellow poet Auden, who presents a sensitive "we" and an ignorant "they." Frost's criticism of life and poetry has always been aimed at snobbish exclusion in all forms. His is the wise courage of honest skepticism, not the false bravado of wishful thinking. He is "acquainted with the night," and he is willing to be "an active doer of whatever is"; yet he is also willing to accept the struggle that has always been sacred for men like him:

> Now let the night be dark for all of me.
> Let the night be too dark for me to see
> Into the future. Let what will be, be.

Still Frost has said that in his own admitted struggle he has never wanted to turn away from any probability. He says that he has always admired the incident in *Pilgrim's Progress* where Pilgrim is asked:

> 'Do you see yon shining gate?'
> 'Yes,' said he, 'I *think* I do.'[2]

So Frost too has his moments when he *thinks* he sees it . . . perhaps "for once, then, something . . ." "But the strong are saying nothing until they know," and Frost's "spiritual drifting" seems as much a deliberate choice in his life today as when he wrote those lines. He still refuses to say without seeing. Though there seems to be in the older Frost a trace of calm, of "anguish transmuted into charity"[3] and peace, he is unable to settle his mind in any such espoused creed of a formal nature as Mauriac and Eliot have.

Suppose he does not find for himself the meaning of the infinite? With the finite still beyond comprehension, his teasing answer is "Why say anything?" In support of his agnosticism, one of his subtitles may be a clue: "Resourcefulness is Next to Understanding." This may be the oldest truth worth renewing to save hearts and minds. Such a defense against confusion is based on knowing what to do with things even though they be tantalizingly incomprehensible, and such resourcefulness has as its object the combining of love and thought into action.

Frost says that he has always admired the heroes of *Walden* and *Robinson Crusoe* for their "limited ability to make snug in the limitless." Such an ability along with a sense of complete freedom makes the dignified isolation which he cherishes as his greatest heritage for his students and readers. Speaking as professor, he commends it to them.

The freedom I'd like to give is the freedom I'd like to have. That is much harder than anything else in the world to get . . . the freedom of my material. . . I think what I'm after is free meditation. . . I would so run a course of self-withdrawal.[4]

It is as a poet of isolation and a teacher of independent thought that Frost would be remembered. He claims to be neither prophet nor saint, and he realizes that man's last stand must be that "of a fighter, not of an orator sawing air." He gives his considered advice—"an endowment to *genus homo*"—with this assurance of the eternal necessity of man's greatest problem:

One can safely say that after six to 30,000 years of experience that the evident design is a situation here in which it will always be about equally hard to save your soul. Whatever progress can be taken to mean, it can't mean making the world any easier a place to save your soul—or if you dislike hearing your soul mentioned in open meeting, say your decency, your integrity. . .[5]

This is as conscientious a stand for Frost today at eighty-eight as when he wrote these words to students thirty-eight years ago. He is still convinced with a kind of Calvinistic fortitude of the necessity of suffering, and he accepts it stoically with good nature as a part of man's human condition.

In the contemporary world where man has never before been more powerful or more fearful, Frost seems to remain calm and fair about this "human condition." He acknowledges man's improvements in what he calls his "domestic science"—the good things brought him by machine; but he realizes that as man has become the master of know-how, he has become less and less capable of reason, wisdom, and love. This poet with his "lover's quarrel with the world" would like to restore what the Ancient Mariner experienced when the ice went out of his soul; to "bless unaware" even an atomic "world he never made" with the wonder and joy of a lover who still finds much of it good. As such, he represents the age-old humanistic tradition in literature that rejects the attempt to describe or account for man wholly on the basis of physics, chemistry, and animal behavior. And this basic humanistic impulse can embrace for Frost the most practical reforms—such as increasing the quality and status of secondary school teachers to which he recently publicly dedicated himself—as well as the most philosophic ones—a search for the calm of a modern Marcus Aurelius that will let him walk as magnanimously as he may in this alien world of the twentieth century. Frost knows that here it is "particularly brave to do anything in the arts" with science in the ascendency; he concludes wistfully, "It's sad to have to be brave, and it takes brains!"[6]

While preparing his most recent book, *In The Clearing*, he remarked, "The great and only event of all history is science plunging deeper into matter. Science has left us all with the great misgiving, this fear that we won't be able to substantiate the spirit."[7] In his urge for this substantiation, Frost may be compared informally to some of the existentialist writers of today. Their philosophic school confronts the human situation. in its totality "to ask what the basic conditions of human existence are and how man can establish his own meaning out of these conditions."[8] To answer the question, they begin with this human existence as a fact without any ready-made preconceptions about the essence of man. Frost too has searched widely and carefully through his poetry for an absolute—"for once, then, something"—about the "one world of any size/That I am like to compass, fool or wise." In many of his seemingly simple animal poems he sees in perspective the fact that man himself is the only animal who not only *can* but *must* ask himself what his existence means. His "theory of opposites" coincides with the existentialists' insistence that no life can be truly enclosed in any system since to exist as an individual at all is to strive, change, develop. Like Kierkegaard, Frost knows that "life is lived forward and understood backward." And he is as sure as are the formal existentialists that it is in the human relationship, not the scientific one, that man must find his real essence. Frost's bravery in the arts leads thus to his bravery in religion—"art belief, then God-belief"—as he originally stated it. He insists that his poetry reflect the truths of pure religion as well as those of pure science from today's world. In his last book, he carefully balances one group entitled "Cluster of Faith" with another called "Quandary." It is significant that he includes his unfinished existential satire "Version" in the former group.

In a recent television appearance Frost seems to speak from an ancient wisdom older than Plato's condemnation of "art as illusion." Here he epitomizes poetically what the existentialists discuss philosophically concerning the essence of our present age:

This present age of ours, I hope, will be found all right for *what it was*. That is, it will have made its point in history. We're going to discriminate once and for all . . . what can and can't be made a science of . . . and we're going to know more about that before we get through this period. That's what it will be remembered for.[9]

159

Frost would be the last to lament and resign himself to the idea that belief in human dignity might be incompatible with scientific knowledge. Like his "West-Running Brook," he knows that the one force depends on the other for support. In "To a Thinker," he teases the pure rationalist and admonishes him neither to blind exaltation nor to empty rejection of reason. With his trust in his instincts as a bard, he knows that the man who exists is, after all, the same man who thinks.

Many of his poems carry another hint of an informal existentialism when they find in the modern conception of man an essence of the tragic hero—whose very dignity comes from a reconciliation of the tragic insight with what is scientifically known. "Design," "Desert Places," "Acquainted with the Night," and even "Happiness Makes up in Height for What It Lacks in Length" all indicate in the preceding explications a personal awareness of the existential situation. "My own desert places" emphasize not so much the far-away fears of an esoteric philosopher nor the immediate warnings of a pragmatic scientist, as the very dignified problem of a man-Poet living here and now, very much aware of his own temporal being and its responsibility for social action. This tragic insight seems to embrace a proud, deliberate self-affirmation that defeats mere determinism. Frost knows that of all the animals, only man can really sense historical time and the precariousness of his own short life in it; yet he is willing to give the lower animals credit for their lesson to man "to make snug in the limitless" in some convenient "cranny or burrow"—to be "resourceful" if he cannot be "understanding." So a hero from Mann, Hemingway, Camus, Joyce, or Pasternak may be justly compared with Frost's "peaceful Shepherd" who looks quietly up for sustenance and chooses "something like a star" for guidance.

In his constant search for self-identification, Frost may also be designated "informally existential." He has said that he owes more to Emerson than to anyone else "for troubled thought,"[10] and yet he is his own man. "I believe in accepting *some* help, but I value myself as a self-helper."[11] He would not, however, impose his standards on others. They must come to their own understanding. Many of his metaphors are closely related to this theme of an individual's necessary pioneering in his own time and history—the "self-belief" that Frost prizes so highly:

I wouldn't want to be urgent about other people's beliefs. (I've never been much for saving the world.) Let them come to them themselves. I never wanted to tell anyone what to believe, but just to start a thought going to see where it comes back.[12]

He would see his own life as the final metaphoric epitome of "the great predicament . . . a figure of a will braving alien entanglements."[13]

160

However, it would obviously be a mistake to envision Frost only as a kind of romantic Don Quixote in his modern universe; he is too much at home in it to lose the Sancho Panza reality of it or to be truly frightened by it.

In his Christmas broadcast of 1955, he acknowledged himself still as "a radical conservative" and insisted that even at eighty the "two roads" looked pretty much the same for all their differences. He is willing, he says today, to risk his attitudes in "the trial by market everything must come to," though he is aware of the fact that today's market is more apt to be a scientific than a poetic one. Still his is a poetry that ends with hope; the tragic wise hope of those who through the ages have outstared the abyss. His own understanding has come from knowing what to do with things, and he has sized up a "world of doubt surrounded" and decided that man himself is the measure of things. He has continued to look "out far" and "in deep." He has concluded: "Poetry is that by which we live forever and ever unjaded; the way to understanding is poetry and mirth."[14]

Predictions for the future of Frost's poetry reveal a mixture of fact and prejudice. Some of the "new critics" have been suspicious of Frost's public popularity. It is true that the Frost personality has often gotten in the way of the poet—the fireside chat in the way of the lyric line—and critics have admonished him for this with reason. Robert Penn Warren accounts for Frost's "too-popular success" in terms of the public's own recognizable error in preferring the man to the poet. Cleanth Brooks suggests that Frost is too often "diluted"—without the intensity that the contemporary world should demand of an artist. Yvor Winters laments Frost's "spiritual drifting" as a dangerous philosophical confusion representative of the general public mind today. R. P. Blackmur complains that Frost has let his craft slip in a way that reflects the lackadaisical tenor of his times. Yet no one of these critics has suggested that Frost's strongest poetry will not outlast his weak age though they find his chief flaws a direct result of it. It is unfortunate that much of the better poetry of Frost has been overlooked by all these critics who are more often critical of Frost's times than of his poetry.

It may be fairly observed, when Frost is accused of being too subjective and personal, that the poets who *have* been retained as classic to our day have generally not been afraid of expressing their personalities. It may also be pointed out that Frost's own age is an age most directly and immediately concerned with fathoming its own depths psychologically and that surely such a tendency can hardly be called old-fashioned.

When Frost is accused of over-cheerfulness in a world of doubt, his critics are seeing only a small segment of his total philosophy and

161

poetry; when he is taken to task for *lack* of spiritual courage, they are not considering obvious historical fact. He has always been happier to be associated with the early "ascending symptoms of *homo sapiens*" than with his more recent pitiful descendings, but he has never suggested the glib optimism and the professional pity of the "positive thinkers." "No tears for the reader; no tears for the writer," he admonishes objectively. He is equally impatient of talk that would insist that this is the best of all possible worlds. "All ages of the world are bad —a great deal worse than Heaven anyway...," and he feels it is presumptuous of man today to think of himself as going down before the worst forces ever mobilized by God.[15] He suggests constantly his theory of opposites to the over-agitated "tendential revolutionists" whom he chides in "The Black Cottage":

> For, dear me, why abandon a belief
> Merely because it ceases to be true.
> Cling to it long enough, and not a doubt
> It will turn true again, and so it goes.
> Most of the change we think we see in life
> Is due to truths being in and out of favor.

Today it is obvious that a good deal of the so-called "philosophic criticism" of Frost is muddled by the contemporary confusion of values. It would seem that Frost's safest claim to fame is through the wiser criticism that examines his poetry for its artistic excellence. He is far happier himself with this latter criticism and recognizes its precision as he ignores the meanderings of the former.

A recent survey of Frost's criticism notes that for over forty years critics have asserted Frost's significance and have valued him highly for certain distinct and recognizable artistic qualities.[16] The continuity of this favorable criticism and its prophecies of permanence have been impressive from the earliest Pound review in 1915, through the Jarrell lectures in 1955, up to the recent essays of John Ciardi and Lawrance Thompson in 1959. Frost has been popular continually with both the serious scholars and the dilettante readers of poetry. The former welcomed him as a new poet who rejected conventionalized form and sentimentalized content, and the latter enjoyed what they thought was happy understanding and hailed him as their own poet-laureate. He has surpassed the limits of regionalism by universalizing his characters; he has avoided the vague abstractions of religious mysticism by an ironic, humorous, and rueful detachment; he has gone beyond the seen to the unseen with a precise metaphysical balance between fact and mystery in his imagery; he has mingled the "sound of sense" with the rhythm of poetry to the benefit of both as the poetic form evolves for both eyes and ears; and he has declared truly that his poetry is at its best when it makes itself as it grows. His artistic peak is reached when the reader's excitement is aroused by the slow unveiling—"the inevitable approach of the moment of complete disclosure."[17]

Though his acclaim is still wide, he has neither stated any new "theory of poetry" nor attracted many young poets as disciples. In an age eager to uproot tradition without offering any substitute, Frost has maintained his centrist position. In this he is not really off the main line of development of modern poetry at all; rather the reverse. He seems to careful critics a representative of the best of both the old and the new:

We may compare his wisdom with that of the last of the Old Ones, Goethe; for we find that it is still possible for that most old-fashioned of old-fashioned things, wisdom, to maintain a marginal existence in our world too.[18]

His greatest wisdom is the wisdom of his own art form, and his clearest expression is in the discipline of its own statement. He knows himself that he is at his best as a practicing artist, not as an amateur philosopher or a lay preacher. He has said that his "one ruthless purpose has been poetry."[19] He has recently expressed what he calls his one constant "personal urgency" after the experience of eighty-eight years of life:

My urgent wish has always been to write two or three poems that will be hard to get rid of . . . what I care about mostly is the "hardness" of the poems. . . so they won't dislodge easily.[20]

In one of his latest poems, Frost casts about looking for a principle of continuity, a metaphor for the source of his strength and wisdom. He wanders up an old country road into a kind of metaphysical past searching for some new "Directive." This directive points to no short-cut to the source; it commands the search and assumes the difficulties without protest through its existence; it is an "essay on love" as the essence of life—love of and on this earth ("I don't know where it's likely to go better"). Its final brevity will be found "outside a house or book," "beginning with delight and ending in wisdom." It has never provided easily-acceptable solutions for this oppositional thinker who continues to substantiate the spirit in spite of "The Great Misgiving." The true source of spiritual strength for Frost is finally found in the great poetic tradition of the past combined with his constant artistic awareness of the present. He would direct others to this same salvation:

> Here are your waters and your watering places;
> Drink and be whole again without confusion.

Footnotes

Preface

[1]Biographies listed chronologically:

   Munson, Gorham B., *Robert Frost: A Study in Sensibility and Good Sense,* New York, George H. Doran, 1927.

   Cox, Sidney, *Robert Frost, Original "Ordinary Man,"* New York, Henry Holt, 1929.

   Cox, Sidney, *A Swinger of Birches: A Portrait of Robert Frost,* New York, New York University Press, 1957.

   Sergeant, Elizabeth Shepley, *Robert Frost: Trial by Existence,* New York, Holt, Rinehart and Winston, Inc., 1960.

Critical Works listed chronologically:

   Thornton, Richard, ed., *Recognition of Robert Frost,* New York, Henry Holt, 1937.

   Thompson, Lawrance, *Fire and Ice,* New York, Henry Holt, 1942.

   Cook, Reginald, *The Dimensions of Robert Frost,* New York, Holt, Rinehart and Winston, Inc., 1958.

   Thompson, Lawrance, *Robert Frost: University of Minnesota Pamphlets on American Writers,* (No. 2), Minneapolis, University of Minnesota Press, 1959.

   Lynen, John F., *The Pastoral Art of Robert Frost,* New Haven, Yale University Press, 1960.

   Nitchie, George W., *Human Values in the Poetry of Robert Frost: A Study of a Poet's Convictions,* Durham, N. C., Duke University Press, 1960.

   Cox, James M., ed. *Robert Frost: A Collection of Critical Essays,* Englewood Cliffs, New Jersey, Prentice-Hall, Inc., 1962.

[2]Allen Tate, ed., *Sixty American Poets—1896-1944,* Washington, D.C., The Library of Congress, 1954.

[3]Robert Frost, "In Winter in the Woods Alone," *In the Clearing,* New York, Holt, Rinehart and Winston, p. 101.

Chapter One

[1]Gorham Munson, *op. cit.,* pp. 1-12.

[2]Joseph Warren Beach, "Robert Frost," *Yale Review,* XLIII, No. 2, (Dec., 1953), pp. 205-208.

[3]Munson, *op. cit.,* pp. 20-25.

[4]Louis and Esther Mertins, *The Intervals of Robert Frost,* Berkeley, The University of California Press, 1947. pp 5-11.

[5]Munson, *op. cit.,* p 28.

⁶Lecture for *Poetry Magazine*, Chicago, Nov. 15. 1955.
⁷Mertins, *op. cit.*, p. 6.
⁸Munson, *op. cit.*, p. 27.
⁹Reginald Cook, "A Time to Listen," *College English*, VII, (Nov. 1945), p. 67.
¹⁰Mertins, *op. cit.*, p. 17.
¹¹James Maurice Thompson in Richard Thornton, *Recognition of Robert Frost, op. cit.*, pp. 17-18.
¹²Reginald Cook, "Robert Frost as Teacher," *College English*, VIII (Feb., 1947), p. 252.
¹³Mertins, *op. cit.*, p. 17.
¹⁴Cook, "Robert Frost as Teacher," *op. cit.*, p. 253.
¹⁵Beach, "Robert Frost," *op. cit.*, p. 208.
¹⁶Munson, *op. cit.*, p. 35.
¹⁷Frost in Munson, *ibid*, p. 43.
¹⁸Beach, "Robert Frost," *op. cit.*, p. 210.
¹⁹Lawrance Thompson, "A Native to the Grain of the American Idiom," *Saturday Review* (March 21, 1959), p. 56.
²⁰Mertins, *op. cit.*, p. 23.
²¹Cook, "Robert Frost as Teacher," *op. cit.*, p. 253.
²²Beach, "Robert Frost," *op cit.*, p. 217.
²³John Bartlett in Munson, *op. cit.*, p. 50.
²⁴Cox, *"Robert Frost, Original "Ordinary Man,"* *op. cit.*, p. 10.
²⁵*Ibid.*
²⁶Mertins, *op. cit.*, p. 26.
²⁷Munson, *op. cit.*, pp. 50-52.
²⁸Pound in Thornton, *op. cit.*, pp. 50-52.
²⁹Mertins, *op. cit.*, p. 28.
³⁰*Ibid.*, pp. 24-29.
³¹Edward Barnett from *The Atlantic Monthly*, in Thornton, *op. cit.*, p. 31.
³²Holt statistics on publications of Frost from Appendix A in Donald E. McCoy's unpublished dissertation, *Robert Frost, Reception and Development of His Poetry*, Urbana, Illinois, The University of Illinois, 1952.
³³Beach, "Robert Frost," *op. cit.*, pp. 208-210.
³⁴Thornton, *op. cit.*, pp. xvii-xx.
³⁵"Robert Frost" in "People, Places, and Things," *Time*, (Sept. 7, 1959). p. 62.
³⁶Thompson, "A Native to the Grain. . ." *op. cit.*, pp. 55-56.
³⁷John Ciardi, "Robert Frost, Master Conversationalist at Work," *Saturday Review*, (March 21, 1959), pp. 17-18.
³⁸Donald Key, "Arts in Iowa," *The Cedar Rapids Gazette*, (April 13, 1959), p. 18.
³⁹Nordell, Rod, "Frost: 'Just a Plain Vert'," *The Christian Science Monitor*, (March 27, 1962), p. 1.
⁴⁰Ciardi, *op. cit.*, p. 18.

Chapter Two

¹Cook. "Frost as Teacher," *op. cit.*, p. 252.
²R.P.T. Coffin, *New Poetry in New England: Robert Frost and Robinson*, Baltimore. The Johns Hopkins Press, 1938, p. 148.
³Frost Lecture for *Poetry Magazine*, Chicago, Nov. 13, 1955.
⁴Frost Lecture at State University of Iowa, Iowa City, April 11, 1959.

[5]Cook, "A Time to Listen," *op. cit.,* p. 77.

[6]Frost in Elizabeth Shepley Sergeant, *Fire under the Andes,* New York, Henry Holt, 1927, p. 310.

[7]Lionel Trilling in Harry Hansen, "Robert Frost Feted for His Poetry," *Chicago Tribune,* Pt. IV, Book Section, (April 5, 1959), p. 13.

[8]Yvor Winters, "Robert Frost, Spiritual Drifter as Poet," *The Sewanee Review, VVI,* (Autumn, 1948), p. 454; also *The Function of Criticism.*

[9]Frost, "The Secret Sits," *Complete Poems,* New York, Henry Holt, 1949, p. 495.

[10]Frost, "Meet the Press," NBC-TV, Dec. 23, 1956.

[11]*Ibid.*

[12]Munson, *op. cit.,* p. 83.

[13]Cook, "Frost as Teacher," *op. cit.,* p. 51

[14]Frost, "Education by Poetry," *Amherst Graduate Quarterly,* XX, No. 2, (Feb., 1931), p. 79.

[15]Frost in Coffin, *op. cit.,* p. 91.

[16]Frost in Cook, "Frost as Teacher," *op. cit.,* p. 250.

[17]Frost in Lecture to Creative Writers' Workshop, State University of Iowa, (April 11, 1959).

[18]Frost, "The Poet's Next of Kin in a College," Princeton, *Biblia,* IX, No. 1, (Feb., 1938), p. 3.

[19]Cook, "Frost as Teacher," *op. cit.,* p. 252.

[20]Sergeant, *op. cit.,* p. 310.

[21]Frost, Introduction to *Mountain Interval,* p. iii.

[22]Arthur Edson, "News Conference with Robert Frost," *The Illinois State Journal,* (Oct. 16, 1958), p. 5.

[23]Frost in conversation with Clyde Tull, Chairman of the English Department, Cornell College, Mt. Vernon, Iowa, 1942.

[24]Sidney Cox, "Robert Frost. . ." *op. cit.,* p. 18.

[25]Beach, "Robert Frost," *op. cit.,* p. 204.

[26]Frost correspondence with Coffin, *op. cit.,* p. 130.

[27]Lecture by Frost in Coffin, *op. cit.,* p. 137.

[28]Thompson, "A Native to the Grain," *op. cit.,* p. 55.

[29]Frost, "One More Brevity," *The Atlantic Monthly,* Vol. 193, (June, 1954), p. 34.

[30]NBC-TV, "Huntley-Brinkley Report," March 26, 1962.

[31]Frost, "The Gift Outright of 'The Gift Outright'," *In The Clearing, op. cit.,* p. 30.

[32]"People, Places, and Things, *Time, op. cit.,* p. 62.

Chapter Three

[1]Donald E. McCoy, *op. cit.,* p. 1.

[2]Thompson, "A Native to the Grain," *op. cit.,* p. 53.

[3]Frost, "Into My Own," *Complete Poems, op. cit.,* p. 5.

[4]Frost, "A Star in a Stone Boat," *Complete Poems, op. cit.,* p. 214.

[5]Frost, "Reluctance," *Complete Poems, op. cit.,* p. 43.

[6]Frost, "Introduction" to *The Memoirs of Stephen Burroughs,* New York, 1924.

[7]Frost, "Introduction" to *A Way Out,* New York, 1929, p i.

[8]Donald Key, "Minority of One," *Cedar Rapids Gazette,* (April 15, 1959), p. 15.

[9]Plato, *Ion,* tr. Lane Cooper, Rinehart, p. 39.

[10]Arthur Edson, *op. cit.,* p. 5.

[11]Plato, *The Republic*, tr. B. Jowett, p. 47.
[12]*Time*, Nov. 4, 1957. p. 63.
[13]Robert Frost, "Open Letter to the Amherst Student," *The Amherst Student*, (March 25, 1935).
[14]Frost, Introduction to *West-Running Brook*, 1939.
[15]Frost in Cook, Reginald, "Robert Frost's Asides," *American Literature*, XIX, (Jan. 1948), p. 354.
[16]Frost, "The Figure a Poem Makes," *op. cit.*, p. vi.
[17]Frost, "A Star in a Stone Boat," *op. cit.*, p. 214.
[18]R. W. Emerson, "The Poet," *Collected Essays*, p. 243.
[19]Arthur Edson, *op. cit.*, p. 5.
[20]Frost, "The Figure a Poem Makes," *op. cit.*, p vi.
[21]Frost, "To a Thinker," *Complete Poems*, p. 431.
[22]Donald Key, "A Minority of One," *op. cit.*, p. 15.
[23]Lawrance Thompson, "A Native to the Grain. . .," *op. cit.*, p. 46.
[24]Donald Key, "A Minority of One," *op. cit.*, p. 15.
[25]Robert Frost, *Complete Poems*, *op. cit.*, p. vi.
[26]Robert Frost, "Small World," NBC-TV, (October 11, 1959).

Chapter Four

[1]Arthur Edson, "News Conference. . ."*op. cit.* p. 5.
[2]Harry Hansen, "Robert Frost Feted. . ." *op. cit.*, p. 13.
[3]Robert Frost in Charles Eliot Norton Lecture at Harvard, 1936.
[4]Robert Frost, Lecture to The New School of Social Research, New York City, 1935.
[5]Reginald Cook, *The Dimensions of Robert Frost*, *op. cit.*, p. 86.
[6]Lawrance Thompson, *Fire and Ice*, *op. cit.*, p. xi.
[7]Frost, "Education by Poetry," *op. cit.*, p. 80.
[8]Samuel T. Coleridge, *Biographia Literaria*, ed. Shawcross, p. 73.
[9]Frost in Cook, "Robert Frost's Asides," *op. cit.*, p. 354.
[10]Frost, "Introduction" to *West-Running Brook*, *op. cit.*, p. iii.
[11]Frost in Cook, "Robert Frost's Asides," *op. cit.*, p. 355.
[12]Frost on "Meet the Press," NBC-TV, Dec. 25, 1955.
[13]Cox, Robert Frost, *Original "Ordinary Man,"* *op. cit.*, p. 56.
[14]Frost, "The Figure a Poem Makes," *op. cit.*, p. v.
[15]Frost, "Poetry and School," *op. cit.*, p. v.
[16]Ciardi, "Robert Frost, Master Conversationalist. . ." *op. cit.*, p. 20.
[17]Frost, "The Figure a Poem Makes," *op. cit.*, p. v.
[18]Frost in Cook, "A Time to Listen," *op. cit.*, p. 66-67.
[19]Frost, "Poetry and School," *op. cit.*, p. 31.
[20]Frost in Thompson, *Fire and Ice*, *op. cit.*, p. 211.
[21]Frost in Cook, "A Time to Listen," *op. cit.*, p. 70.
[22]Frost, "The Figure a Poem Makes," *op. cit.*, p. vi.
[23]Thompson, *Fire and Ice*, *op. cit.*, p. 23.
[24]Frost, "The Figure a Poem Makes," *op. cit.*, pp. vi-vii.
[25]Ciardi, "Robert Frost, Master Conversationalist," *op. cit.*, p. 18.
[26]Frost in Munson, *op. cit.*, p. 83.
[27]Ciardi, "Robert Frost, Master Conversationalist," *op. cit.*, p. 18.
[28]Frost in Cook, *The Dimensions of Robert Frost*, p. 79.
[29]Frost in Lecture, State University of Iowa, April 13, 1959.
[30]Frost in Ciardi, *op. cit.*, p. 20.
[31]Frost in Cook, *Dimensions of Robert Frost*, p. 66.
[32]Frost in Ciardi, *op. cit.*, p. 20.

[33]Frost in Creative Writers' Workshop, State University of Iowa, April 13, 1959.

[34]Frost in David L. Norton, "Bigger Than His Work," *St. Louis Post-Dispatch*, (March 16, 1959), p. 18.

[35]Frost in Cook, "A Time to Listen," *op. cit.*, p. 70.

[36]Frost in Oscar Williams, *A Little Treasury of Modern Poetry*, New York, Scribners, 1952, p. 798.

[37]J. Donald Adams, "Speaking of Books," *New York Times*, Book Section, (March 22, 1959), p. 2.

[38]Donald Key, "The Arts in Iowa," *op. cit.*, p. 17.

Chapter Five

[1]Frost in Thompson, *op. cit.*, p. 41.

[2]Robert Frost, "The Poetry of Amy Lowell," *Christian Science Monitor*, (May 16, 1925), p. 31.

[3]Robert Frost, "A Poet's Next of Kin in a College," *op. cit.*, p. 2.

[4]These themes take three major forms: lyric, dramatic, satiric. The term "satire" here and in Chapter X is used to include a wide variety of genres from didactic sermon and rhymed editorial to whimsical fable and taut epigram. All poetry quoted is from Frost's *Complete Poems* (1949), with the permission of the publisher, Henry Holt.

[5]Cleanth Brooks, *Modern Poetry and the Tradition*, Chapel Hill, 1939, p. 65.

[6]Frost in Thompson, *op. cit.*, p. 20.

[7]Frost in Donald Adams, "Speaking of Books," *op. cit.* (Nov. 1, 1959).

[8]Frost in correspondence with R. P. T. Coffin, *op. cit.*, p. 137.

[9]Randall Jarrell, "The Other Robert Frost," *The Nation*, CLXVI, (Nov. 27, 1947), p. 590.

[10]Frost, "Not All There," *Complete Poems*, p. 408.

[11]Frost, "In Hardwood Groves," *Complete Poems*, p. 37.

[12]Frost, "A Passing Glimpse," *Complete Poems*, p. 311.

[13]Randall Jarrell, "The Other Robert Frost," *op. cit.*, p. 600. (Jarrell here calls Frost "the best poet on isolation since Matthew Arnold.")

[14]Yvor Winters, "Robert Frost, The Spiritual Drifter as Poet," *op. cit.*; H. H. Waggoner, *The Heel of Elohim*, *op. cit.*, pp. 54-60.

[15]Mary Elizabeth Smith, "The Function of Natural Phenomena in the Poetry of Robert Frost," unpublished dissertation at the University of Iowa, Iowa City, (June, 1951).

[16]R. W. Emerson, "The American Scholar," in Foerster, *Backgrounds of American Literature*, p. 475.

[17]Frost in Thompson, *Fire and Ice*, p. 51.

[18]Frost, "Education by Poetry," *op. cit.*, p. 80.

[19]Frost, "Poetry and School," *op. cit.*, p. 30.

[20]Mary Elizabeth Smith, *op. cit.*, p. 8.

[21]Frost, "Education by Poetry," *op. cit.*, p. 81.

[22]Mary Elizabeth Smith, *op. cit.*, p. 19.

[23]Milton Bracker, "Capitol Honors Frost," *New York Times* (March 26, 1962).

[24]Frost in Cook, "A Time to Listen," *op. cit.*, p. 168.

[25]Yvor Winters, "Robert Frost, The Spiritual Drifter as Poet," *op. cit.*, p. 568.

[26]Frost, "Education by Poetry," *op. cit.*, p. 77.

[27]Frost, "But God's Own Descent," *op. cit.*, p. 7.

Chapter Six

[1]Frost in Cook, "Robert Frost's Asides," *op. cit.*, p. 68.
[2]*Ibid.*
[3]Frost, "The Poetry of Amy Lowell," *op. cit.*, p. 13.
[4]Frost in Cook, "Robert Frost's Asides," *op. cit.*, p. 70.
[5]Frost in "Meet the Press," NBC-TV, Dec. 25, 1955.
[6]Frost in Coffin, *op. cit.*, p. 381.
[7]Frost in Cook, "A Time to Listen," *op. cit.*, p. 168.
[8]Frost in lecture at Bread Loaf School of English, Aug. 18, 1945.
[9]Frost, "The Figure a Poem Makes," *op. cit.*, p. vii.
[10]Coffin, *op. cit.*, p. 82.
[11]Willard Thorp, *Literary History of the United States* (ed. R. Spiller, *et al*), 1948, p. 521.
[12]Thompson, *Fire and Ice, op. cit.*, pp. 72-86.
[13]*Ibid.*, p. 72.
[14]Frost in Cook, "A Time to Listen," *op. cit.*, p. 68.
[15]Frost in Introduction to E. A. Robinson, *King Jaspar*, New York, 1935, p. iv.
[16]Frost in Introduction to *A Way Out, op. cit.*, p. iii.
[17]Frost in Braithwaite, Stanley, "Robert Frost, New American Poet," *Boston Evening Transcript* (May 6, 1915), p. 4.
[18]Frost in J. Donald Adams, "Speaking of Books," *New York Times* Book Section (Nov. 8, 1959), p. 19.
[19]R. W. Emerson, *Collected Poems*, p. 93.
[20]Frost, "Education by Poetry," *op. cit.*, p. 82.
[21]Frost in Beach, "Robert Frost," *op. cit.*, p. 207.
[22]Frost in Cook, "A Time to Listen," p. 69.
[23]McCoy, *op. cit.*, pp. 190-200.
[24]Thornton, "Four Prefaces to a Book," *Recognition of Robert Frost, op. cit.*, pp. 293-307.
[25]Frost, "The Figure a Poem Makes," *op. cit.*, p. vii.
[26]Frost in R. L. Newdick, "Robert Frost and the Dramatic," *New England Quarterly*, X (June, 1927), pp. 262-269.
[27]Frost in Introduction to *A Way Out*, p. vi.
[28]Frost in Coffin, *op. cit.*, pp. 100-104.
[29]Randall Jarrell, "To the Laodiceans," *Kenyon Review*, (Autumn, 1952), p. 550.
[30]H. H. Waggoner, *The Heel of Elohim, op. cit.*, p. 56.
[31]Frost in Cook, *The Dimensions of Robert Frost, op. cit.*, p. 58.

Chapter Seven

[1]Thompson, *Fire and Ice, op. cit.*, p. 57.
[2]Frost, Introduction to Robinson's *King Jaspar, op. cit.*, p. viii.
[3]Brooks and Warren, *Understanding Poetry*, New York, 1950, p. 115.
[4]Randall Jarrell, "The Other Robert Frost," *op. cit.*, p. 575.
[5]Thompson, *Fire and Ice, op. cit.*, p. 113.
[6]Frost in Cox, *Swinger of Birches, op. cit.*, p. 20.
[7]Frost in "Meet the Press," NBC-TV, (Dec. 25, 1955).
[8]Frost in "Small World," NBC-TV, (October 11, 1959).
[9]Frost letter to R. P. T. Coffin, *op. cit.*, p. 145.
[10]H. H. Waggoner, *op. cit.*, p. 57; Peter Viereck, "Parnassus Divided," *The Atlantic Monthly*, 184 (Oct. 1949), p. 68; Mark Van Doren, "Robert

Frost's America," *The Atlantic Monthly*, 187 (June, 1951), p. 39.
[11]Frost in Coffin, *op. cit.*, p. 79.
[12]Frost in Waggoner, *op. cit.*, p. 48.
[13]Frost in Coffin, *op. cit.*, p. 80.
[24]Milton Bracker, "Capitol Honors Frost," *op. cit.*

PART III: Chapters Eight, Nine, Ten
His Poetry: Lyrics, Dramatic Narratives, Satires

[1]Randall Jarrell, "To the Laodiceans," *op. cit.*, p. 537.
[2]All poems quoted from *The Complete Poems of Robert Frost*, New York,
Henry Holt, 1949, with the permission of the publishers.

Conclusion

[1]Frost in Cox, *Original "Ordinary" Man*, *op. cit.*, p. 148.
[2]Frost in Thompson, *Fire and Ice*, p. 206.
[3]François Mauriac ,"The Final Answer," *Saturday Evening Post* (Dec. 5,
1959), p. 65.
[4]Frost, "The Manumitted Student," *New Student*, VI (Jan. 12, 1927), p. 1.
[5]Frost, "Open Letter to the Amherst Student," *op. cit.*, p. 4.
[6]Frost in Ciardi, "Master Conversationalist at Work," *op. cit.*, p. 17.
[7]*Ibid.*
[8]Wm. L. Barrett, "What is Existentialism?" *Saturday Evening Post* (Nov.
21, 1959), p. 45.
[9]*Ibid.*
[10]Frost in J. Donald Adams, "Speaking of Books," *New York Times* Book
Section (March 22, 1959), p. 3.
[11]Frost in Ciardi, "Master Conversationalist at Work," *op. cit.*, p. 19.
[12]*Ibid.*
[13]Frost, "The Figure a Poem Makes," *op. cit.*, p. viii.
[14]Frost in "Meet the Press," NBC-TV, (Dec. 25, 1955).
[15]Frost in "Open Letter to the Amherst Student," *op. cit.*, p. 4.
[16]McCoy, *op. cit.*, pp. 240-256.
[17]Thorp in Spiller, *et al. Literary History of the United States*, p. 119.
[18]Randall Jarrell, "To the Laodiceans," *op. cit.*, p. 561.
[19]J. Donald Adams, "Speaking of Books," *New York Times* Book Section
(March 22, 1959), p. 3.
[20]Frost in Ciardi, "Master Conversationalist at Work," *op. cit.*, p. 54.
[21]Frost, "Directive," *Complete Poems, op. cit.*, p. 520.

Selected Bibliography

Primary Sources

Frost, Robert, *The Complete Poems of Robert Frost*, New York: Henry
    Holt and Company, 1949.
————, ————, "Education by Poetry," *The Amherst Graduates' Quarterly*,
    XX (February, 1931), 2.
————, ————, *In The Clearing*, New York: Holt, Rinehart and Winston, Inc.,
    1962.
————, ————, "Open Letter to Amherst Students," *The Amherst Students'
    Magazine*, XXI (March 25, 1935), 4.
————, ————, "Poetry and School," *The Atlantic Monthly*, CLXXXVII
    (June, 1951), 30-31.
————, ————, "The Poet's Next of Kin in a College," *Princeton Biblia*, IX
    (February, 1938), 3.

Secondary Sources

Baker, Carlos, "Frost on the Pumpkin," *Georgia Review*, XI (Summer,
    1957), 117-31.
Beach, Joseph Warren, "Robert Frost," *Yale Review*, XLIII (December,
    1953), 205-08.
Brooks, Cleanth, and Robert P. Warren, *Conversations with Robert Frost on
    the Craft of Poetry*, New York: Holt, Rinehart and Winston, Inc., 1961.
Booth, Phillip, "Journey Out of a Dark Forest," *New York Times Book
    Review* (March 25, 1962), 1.
Ciardi, John, "Robert Frost: American Bard," *Saturday Review*, XLV
    (March 24, 1962), 15-17.
Ciardi, John, "Robert Frost: Master Conversationalist at Work," *Saturday
    Review*, XLII (March 21, 1959), 17-18.
Coffin, R. P. T., *New Poetry in New England: Robert Frost and E. A.
    Robinson*, Baltimore: Johns Hopkins Press, 1938.
Cook, Reginald, *The Dimensions of Robert Frost*, New York: Holt, Rine-
    hart and Winston, Inc., 1958.
Cook, Reginald, "Robert Frost's Asides on His Poetry," *American Literature*,
    XIX (January, 1949), 351-59.
Cook, Reginald, "Robert Frost as Teacher," *College English*, VIII (February,
    1947), 252-55.
Cook, Reginald, "A Time to Listen," *College English*, VII (November,
    1945), 66-77.
Cowley, Malcolm, "The Case Against Mr. Frost," *The New Republic*, CXI
    (September 11 and 18, 1944), 312-14 and 345-47.
Cox, James M., *Robert Frost: A Collection of Critical Essays*, Englewood
    Cliffs, New Jersey: Prentice-Hall, Inc., 1962.
Cox, James M., "Robert Frost and the Edge of the Clearing," *Virginia
    Quarterly Review*, XXXV (Winter, 1959), 73-88.

Cox, Sidney, "Robert Frost and the Poetic Fashion," *The American Scholar,* XVII (Winter, 1948-49), 78-86.

Cox, Sidney, *Robert Frost, Original "Ordinary Man,"* New York: Henry Holt, 1929.

Cox, Sidney, *A Swinger of Birches; A Portrait of Robert Frost,* New York: New York University Press, 1957.

Hopkins, Vivian C., "Robert Frost: Out Far and In Deep," *Western Humanities Review,* XIV (Summer, 1960), 247-63.

Jarrell, Randall, "The Other Robert Frost," *The Nation,* CLXV (November 27, 1947), 588-92.

Jarrell, Randall, "To the Laodiceans," *Kenyon Review* (Autumn, 1952), 535-56.

Lowell, Amy, "Robert Frost," in *Poets and Their Art,* New York: The Macmillan Company, 1926, 56-62.

Lynen, John F., *The Pastoral Art of Robert Frost,* New Haven, Connecticut: Yale University Press, 1960.

Montgomery, Marion, "Robert Frost and His Use of Barriers," *The South Atlantic Quarterly,* LVII (Summer, 1958), 339-53.

Munson, Gorham, *Robert Frost: A Study in Sensibility and Good Sense,* New York: George H. Doran, 1927.

Napier, John T., "A Momentary Stay Against Confusion," *The Virginia Quarterly Review,* XXXIII (Summer, 1957), 378-94.

Nitchie, George W., *Human Values in the Poetry of Robert Frost,* Durham, North Carolina: Duke University Press, 1960.

O'Donnell, W. G., "Robert Frost and New England, A Revaluation," *The Yale Review* (Summer, 1948), 698-712.

Ogilvie, John T., "From Woods to Stars: A Pattern of Imagery in Robert Frost's Poetry," *South Atlantic Quarterly,* LVIII (Winter, 1959), 64-76.

Pearce, Roy Harvey, "Frost's Momentary Stay," *Kenyon Review,* XXIII (Spring, 1961), 258-73.

Poirier, Richard, "The Art of Poetry: Robert Frost," *The Paris Review,* 24 (Summer-Fall, 1960), 88-120.

Sergeant, Elizabeth Shepley, *Robert Frost: Trial by Existence,* New York: Holt, Rinehart and Winston, Inc., 1960.

Thompson, Lawrance, *Fire and Ice,* New York: Henry Holt, 1942.

Thompson, Lawrance, "A Native to the Grain of the American Idiom," *Saturday Review,* XLII (March 21, 1959), 56-60.

Thompson, Lawrance, *Robert Frost,* Minneapolis, Minnesota: University of Minnesota Press, 1959.

Thornton, Richard, *Recognition of Robert Frost,* New York: Henry Holt, 1937.

Trilling, Lionel, "A Speech on Robert Frost: A Cultural Episode," *The Partisan Review,* XXVI (Summer, 1959), 445-52.

Untermeyer, Louis, *The Pocket Book of Robert Frost,* New York: Washington Square Press, 1946.

Van Doren, Mark, "Robert Frost's America," *The Atlantic Monthly,* 187 (June, 1951), 39-42.

Viereck, Peter, "Parnassus Divided," *The Atlantic Monthly,* 185 (October, 1949), 68-71.

Watts, Harold H., "Robert Frost and the Interrupted Dialogue," *American Literature,* XXVII (March, 1955), 69-87.

Winters, Yvor, "Robert Frost, Spiritual Drifter as Poet," *The Function of Criticism,* Denver: Alan Swallow, 1956.